# THE PERFECT RESUME

*Resumes That Work in The New Economy!*

*2nd Edition*

## Dan Quillen

Author of *Get a Job!*, *The Perfect Interview*, *Your First Job*, and

*Use Social Media to Get Your Dream Job!*

"I felt like the author was coaching me personally as I read through the book."

*– Nadine Newell*

*The Perfect Resume-- Resumes That Work in the New Economy* is the second in the Get a Job! series of books written by Dan Quillen. Quillen calls on his expertise as an HR professional (and as one who lost and found a job in the toughest economic environment since the Great Depression) to help his readers understand the New Economy, and how to find work when many cannot.

In this book, Dan focuses on that most important tool in a job hunter's quiver: the resume. Quillen walks you through the technical aspects of resume writing, but also helps you to understand the tricks of the resume-writing trade. He shows you how to write resumes that end up in the hands of hiring managers – not screened by gatekeepers and deposited in the recycle bin.

## CITATIONS

Lies, damned lies and statistics quote: *en.wikipedia.org/wiki/Lies,_damned_lies,_and_ statistics*

Thomas Edison quote: *www.brainyquote.com/quotes/quotes/t/thomasaed131294.html*

John F. Kennedy quote: *www.brainyquote.com/quotes/quotes/j/johnfkenn103820.html*

Lily Tomlin quote: *www.brainyquote.com/quotes/quotes/l/lilytomlin379145.html*

Mark Twain quote (Difference between the right and wrong word): *www.brainyquote.com/ quotes/quotes/m/marktwain389874.html*

Billy Zane quote: *www.brainyquote.com/quotes/quotes/b/billyzane443043.html*

Nelson Mandela quote: *www.brainyquote.com/quotes/quotes/n/nelsonmand121685.html*

Dave Eggers quote: *www.brainyquote.com/quotes/quotes/d/daveeggers484224.html*

Albert Einstein quote: *www.brainyquote.com/quotes/quotes/a/alberteins102068.html*

Paul Johnson quote: *www.brainyquote.com/quotes/quotes/p/pauljohnso549966.html*

Charles Dickens quote: *www.brainyquote.com/quotes/quotes/c/charlesdic106118.html*

Norman Vincent Peale quote: *www.brainyquote.com/quotes/quotes/n/normanvinc132560. html*

Mark Twain quote (Truth): *www.brainyquote.com/quotes/quotes/m/marktwain118210.html*

Plato quote: *www.brainyquote.com/quotes/quotes/p/plato398609.html*

Wayne Gretzsky quote: *www.brainyquote.com/quotes/quotes/w/waynegretz378694.html*

Bob Weinstein quote: *www.brainyquote.com/quotes/quotes/b/bobweinste242897.html*

Alexander Graham Bell quote: *www.brainyquote.com/quotes/quotes/a/alexanderg389638. html*

# PRAISE FOR DAN'S BOOKS

"I was out of work for almost 2 years, and was just not getting many responses from the resumes I was sending out. I picked up a copy of Dan's book and began following his counsel in a number of areas, especially related to resumes and interviewing. Within 3 weeks, I had 4 interviews and received two job offers. I am now happily employed with a great job and feel like following Dan's counsel is the primary reason I was able to get these job offers and land my job." – *Jeremy Savage*

"Dan Quillen knows what he is talking about in this book. I took his advice and had a job within 3 weeks of being laid off. Buy it today and it will set you on a direct course to success!" – *Lynette W. Fox*

"Mr. Quillen's book is an easy read with a great deal of helpful information. Having been a hiring manager and HR director, as well as having been laid off himself during the recent recession, Mr. Quillen has a particular expertise that others may not. This book is also written with a focus on how techniques in job searching have changed in recent years, due to technology and the economy. I highly recommend this book to those that are either newly unemployed or wishing to make a change." – *Debra S. Heglin*

"If you want to spend your money wisely on creating a résumé that will result in interviews and therefore job offers, this book will take you further and more expeditiously than most so-called experts. He gives clear, simple, succinct direction in *Get a Job!* to create a résumé that will get the interview to get the job! Don't skip any chapters!" – *Ginny Ford, Ford Personnel, Inc.*

"I have been recommending *The Perfect Resume* to all my candidates for the past month. I loved the content and the order of things that you spoke about." – *Sally S. Cohen, President, The Arundel Group*

# COLD SPRING PRESS
*www.get-a-great-job.com*

Copyright © 2016 by W. Daniel Quillen
ISBN 13: 978-1-59360-222-2
Library of Congress Control Number: 2016948030

PHOTO CREDITS: p. 17, David Monniaux from Wikimedia Commons

## ABOUT THE AUTHOR

**Dan Quillen** is the author of *Get a Job! – How I Found a Job When Jobs are Hard to Find, And So Can You!, The Perfect Resume, The Perfect Interview, Your First Job* and *Use Social Media to Find Your Dream Job!* He has been a professional in Human Resources for more than twenty years. For a decade, he was the Director of Human Resources for one of the largest law firms in the western United States. Currently he is the Director of Internal Services (managing Human Resources, Purchasing, Risk and Fleet) for the City of Aurora, the third largest city in Colorado.

For years, Dan has been an active mentor for those who are out of work, freely sharing his expertise in résumé review and creation, interviewing and job searching. A few years ago Dan was laid off and had the opportunity to try the techniques he has been teaching others for years. In all of Dan's books, he shares the knowledge and techniques that allowed him to find a job in a short period of time during the worst economic downturn our country has had since the Great Depression.

When not doing HR, Dan is a professional writer specializing in travel, technical, genealogy, and how-to subjects. He has written and published 18 books on various topics. Dan makes his home in Centennial, Colorado. If you'd like to contact Dan about anything in this book, his e-mail address is: wdanielquillen@gmail.com, and he welcomes your comments and questions.

# Table of Contents

# THE PERFECT RESUME

*Resumes That Work in The New Economy!*

 **Introduction**

Thank you for purchasing *The Perfect Resume – Resumes That Work in the New Economy*. If you've purchased this book, or checked it out from the library, or it has been given to you by a friend or family member, it probably means you are out of work or working and looking for a change. Either way, you are looking for work, and you have correctly surmised that a winning resume – the Perfect Resume, shall we say? – is essential to your success.

The **New Economy** means that more people are unemployed, and more people under-employed than at any time since the Great Depression – eight decades ago! And while the government trumpets record-low unemployment rates, it's because they have stopped counting those who have been out of work a certain amount of time. And while the economy is improving somewhat (even though it is still terribly fragile!), the percentage of American workers in the workforce is the lowest it has been since the Great Depression.

In this New Economy, even though we are seeing fewer applicants per job than during the heart of the Great Recession (when there were hundreds of applicants for jobs), we are seeing much more qualified applicants. It means that hiring managers and Human Resources departments are understaffed compared to just a few years ago, so they have turned to applications software to screen the majority of resumes and applications down to a manageable number that can be reviewed personally.

So what the New Economy really means is that job hunters have to be savvy. They have to be qualified. They have to be persistent. They have to know how to present themselves to overcome those obstacles.

And that's what this book is all about.

Naturally, you may have a few questions about this book. There are a number of books about resumes on the market – what makes this one different? Why should you purchase it, or listen to what it has to say? Let's see if I can answer those and other questions you may have:

**What qualifies this guy to write this book?**

I have been a Human Resource professional for over two decades, and for longer than that, I have been a hiring manager. I know what hiring managers and HR departments look for when screening applicants and resumes for positions. And – perhaps more important – I know what works and what does not work for applicants when it comes to resumes.

**Does this guy know anything about finding work in the New Economy?**

Yes – several years ago, at the height of the Recession, I found myself suddenly out of work. I walked the path you are walking, and I know what it takes to get my resume in front of hiring managers, and to earn an interview. I have done it, and I have done it in the New Economy. During my short time as an unemployed worker, I applied for 130 positions. I was successful in getting 31 interviews – nearly a one-in-four hit rate. I succeeded in getting that ratio of interviews when my peers were getting one interview for every 20 or 25 resumes they submitted. Through the pages of this book, I will share how you can also have that kind of success.

**Why is this guy writing this book?**

I have to be honest (I always am!) – it appalls me to see how little so many candidates know about searching for jobs. It is almost stunning to see the naïveté of many job searchers on an almost daily basis. That was one of the reasons I wrote *Get a Job!* – the first in this series of books about finding a job in the New Economy, and why I have written this follow-on book about resumes.

## INTRODUCTION

My hope is that through the pages of this book you can learn a few key principles to crafting a successful resume, one that not only looks good, but one that works.

**This guy knows what he's talking about!**

I am interested to hear how things are going in your job search. When you have a chance, please e-mail me at *wdanielquillen@gmail.com* and let me know how it is going, your successes, and even some of your questions.

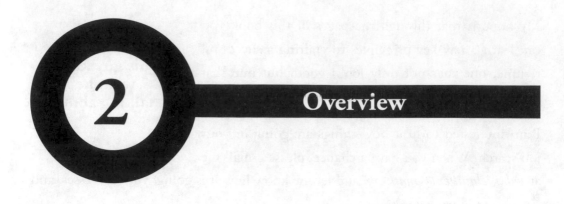

**2**      Overview

*Believe in yourself! Have faith in your abilities! Without a humble but reasonable confidence in your own powers you cannot be successful or happy.*
– Norman Vincent Peale

Thank you for your interest in *The Perfect Resume*! Over the next several hundred pages, we'll spend a little time together, discussing information you should know about resumes. I have reviewed literally tens of thousands of resumes through the years, and have some definite opinions on what works – and what does not! So if you'll read on, you'll learn more about what will work for you in your job search.

This is a tough economy – the toughest in over eight decades, since the Great Depression. So many Americans are out of work, and most jobs these days have scores of qualified applicants. You need to find a way to be noticed as a candidate, and your resume is the starting point for accomplishing that.

In **Chapter 1**, *Introduction*, we'll talk about the toxic New Economy, and I will outline my credentials that allow me to write this book – not only my two-plus decades of HR work, but the fact that I lost my job during this New Economy, and was able to find a new job within a very short time.

In **Chapter 3**, *The Importance of a Resume,* we'll debunk the myth that you can find work without a professional resume. We'll explore what you need to do to capture a hiring manager's interest.

# OVERVIEW

In **Chapter 4**, *The Mechanics of Resume Writing*, we'll explore the elements required to write a successful resume. We'll talk about resume shorthand, the language you should use in your resume. We'll talk about how to handle acronyms effectively, and what kind of formatting to use to make your resume prominent among the hundreds of others with which you are competing. We'll learn how to present a crisp, clean and professional look and feel with your resume.

In **Chapter 5**, *Key Words and Action Words*, I will present the concept of making certain the key words you use in your resume are those that will likely get your resume through the screeners and onto the hiring manager's desk. We'll speak briefly about action / power words – words you can use to enliven your resume and spice it up a bit. And – we'll talk about where you can find resources for key words and action words.

In **Chapter 6**, *List Your Accomplishments*, we'll talk about a critical element that is left out of probably 90% of the resumes out there these days. Accomplishments help hiring managers understand not only what you did, but how well you did it. In this New Economy, you must stand out among the competition in order to earn your position. One way to do that is to quantify the success you had in previous jobs, rather than simply provide a list of tasks and responsibilities (like everyone else does). This will help you differentiate yourself from the competition.

In **Chapter 7**, *Appearance Matters*, I will help you understand the difference between a vanilla / ho-hum presentation of your resume and one that impresses hiring managers and those who are responsible for screening resumes. This is an area you simply must pay attention to as you assemble your resume.

In **Chapter 8**, *Resume Language*, we'll spend a short amount of time helping you understand the proper language to use in your resume. We'll make sure you understand the language you are to speak in your resume so you look like a professional and not an amateur.

In **Chapter 9**, *Resume Formats*, I will share with you the three basic formats for resumes: Functional, Chronological and a Combination Functional / Chronological resume. I will share the relative strengths and weaknesses of each type format, and provide you with my recommendation for the type of resume format you should use. At the end of the day, of course, you must feel comfortable with the format you choose for your own resume.

In **Chapter 10**, *One Size Doesn't Fit All!*, we'll talk about the absolute necessity of tailoring your resume for every position to which you apply. What's at stake here? You can languish along at getting one interview for every twenty or so resumes you submit, or you can increase your chances four to five fold. Success in tailoring your resume results in more interviews, and more interviews result in quicker job offers.

In **Chapter 11**, *The Dead Moose on the Table (How to Handle Resume Difficulties)*, we discuss what you need to do to overcome the most common dead moose on the table – including little or no experience, gaps in employment, lack of education and issues pertaining to older workers and younger workers. If you are facing any of these difficulties, you must have a strategy of how to overcome those thorny issues.

In **Chapter 12**, *Section-by-Section Resume Review*, we'll stroll through the crucial elements and sections you have to have in your resume for it to be successful. Along the way, I'll share my expertise and thoughts for each section, and you'll learn what needs to go within each section – and what sections shouldn't be included in professional resumes.

In **Chapter 13**, *Resume Samples*, I'll bring the information from all the previous chapters together and provide you with a half dozen examples of resumes you can use as templates / guidelines for your own resume.

In **Chapter 14**, *Letters of Recommendation*, I'll talk about an element of resume packages that is often overlooked. Letters of recommendation are often used by hiring managers to learn more about the candidates they are considering. These letters of recommendation may be the slight edge you need that will make the difference between winning the role and coming in second place.

# OVERVIEW

In **Chapter 15**, *A Baker's Dozen Of Resume Errors*, I'll share a gaggle of resume gaffes I run across frequently, and will help you understand that you cannot afford to commit any of these resume transgressions.

In **Chapter 16**, *Miscellany*, I cover a hodge podge of topics that just didn't seem to fit anyplace else, but that I think are important considerations for you. I speak about the importance of good references, moms re-entering the workforce, felons re-entering the workforce, and I share a way not to use your resume!

In **Chapter 17**, *In Closing*, I provide you with some last thoughts about crafting a professional resume that will help you end your unemployment.

At the end of each chapter, I have provided you with a checklist, sort of a summary of what was covered in the chapter, and a reminder of things you should – and should not – do to be successful in your job hunt.

So let's go. Strap on your job-search seatbelt, and let's figure out how you can make this chapter in your life as short as possible!

# 3 The Importance of a Resume

*What's in a name? That which we call a rose by any other name would smell as sweet.*
(Juliet to Romeo, *Romeo and Juliet*, William Shakespeare)

I recently saw the title of a book that made me uneasy. It was something like: *The Resume is Dead!*

Don't you believe that. If you are looking for a job without a resume, you are in trouble. It's like fishing without a pole, hook, bait or net, like flying without a plane. Like them or not, like your resume or not, you will still be faced with the necessity of putting one together if you are to find and accept a new job.

When I lost my job in the middle of the Recession, I applied for 130 jobs. Every single one of them required a resume. Every single one of them expected me to provide a resume – whether I was asked to cut and paste it, upload it, scan it or fax it, mail it or deliver it by Pony Express rider (okay – maybe not that last option!). The most basic request was for me to provide a resume. It serves as the foundation of your job search. Don't take the chance of having a shaky foundation.

But – a resume isn't a resume isn't a resume. There are many types of resumes, many different formats, looks, feels, approaches, etc. Following are a few of the basic functions of your resume; it must:

> • provide information about your experience;

- lay out your skills in an interesting and easily readable format;

- show not only what you did, but how you did it;

- look professional;

- pique a hiring manager's interest.

Let's talk briefly about each of those resume duties.

**Provide Information About Your Experience**

Your resume must provide hiring managers, HR departments and recruiters with a concise and accurate summary of the work you have done. It is your "me in thirty seconds" / "elevator speech" on paper. Unfortunately you won't have the opportunity to turn your personal charm on every person who will be evaluating you for a position within their company. So your resume must be clear, concise and to the point. It can't wander around or obscure important facts about you and your career.

**Lay Out Your Skills in an Interesting and Readable Format**

As you begin your resume, one of your main goals should be to make things as easy on your resume's reviewers as you can. Pull out important items so they will see them rapidly and can identify them as important to them and the position they are trying to fill. What you don't want is to force hiring managers, recruiters and HR departments to have to search through your resume with a fine-tooth comb, searching for things that might be important to them and the position they have open.

**Show What You Did, And How Well You Did it**

Later, in the Accomplishments chapter, you'll learn the importance of including *accomplishments* as well as how to identify accomplishments that might not be readily apparent to you as you put your resume

**Will my resume pique a hiring manager's interest?**

together. This is an area that is overlooked by far too many job seekers. I would guess that fewer than 10% of job seekers – even for professional jobs – do a good job of identifying accomplishments on their resumes or in their cover letters.

Accomplishments tell the hiring manager not only what you did, but how well you did it. They allow you to tell how you made a difference, how you were exceptional at your job. Accomplishments take on a number of forms: you might share awards and recognition, promotions, improvements you made, savings you earned for the company, etc., etc.

Some accomplishments are more difficult to identify than others. Sales or manufacturing jobs tend to lend themselves more to accomplishments than other jobs: percent of quota obtained, monetary volume of sales you did, number of widgets produced, etc. But I have spent the last twenty+ years in a field that sometimes makes it difficult to identify accomplishments: Human Resources. And there are many jobs out there like that. I don't sell any products, or increase revenues that I can point to as evidence of success. I can't say, "Well, I saved the company 15 million dollars because no one sued us for that amount because when I terminated their employment, I did it correctly." But I must still look for ways to demonstrate that I was better than the Average Joe in doing my job. To the extent I can do that, I will be more successful in my job hunt. (Be sure to spend time with chapter 6!)

**Look Professional**

Your resume must look professional – when someone glances at it, even before they read a single word, you want your resume to shout:

> Professional! Organized! Capable! Competent!

And how do you that? You lay it out in an organized and methodical manner. Information is easy to find. The things you have done that match the job requirements are front and center. You use plenty of white space – space at the top, bottom and side margins of your resume, space between resume entries, sections, etc. – it doesn't look cramped. You have provided information in bite-size pieces – instead of paragraphs of prose, you provide bullet-pointed entries that are quick and easy to read.

You've probably heard the story about the presenter who was demonstrating how to make effective presentations. (Even if you have already heard this story, it's worth a review in this context.) She presented a lovely chocolate cake she had baked to the audience, and asked if anyone wanted a piece of cake. Many (most!) hands in the audience went up, and she selected one volunteer. She asked the volunteer to come up to the front with her.

Once the volunteer arrived, she pulled out a paper plate, stretched her hand out and grabbed a glob of cake, then plopped it on the plate. The audience and the volunteer were amazed and not a little stunned. The cake looked anything but appetizing.

Then the presenter invited another volunteer up to join her. She set out a Wedgwood china plate, and positioned a beautiful silver fork next to the plate. She then got out a large, sharp knife and turned the cake around, slicing a piece from the undamaged side of the cake. She placed it on the china plate, and presented it to the volunteer.

Her point, of course, was that presentation is important. And so it is with your resume. If your resume is cramped, looks like a term paper because you've used such a small font, it is akin to the first piece of chocolate cake mentioned above.

On the other hand, if your resume has an attractive appearance, if the first words the screener's eyes fall upon happen to be skills they are seeking, then your resume is the piece of cake on the Wedgwood china plate – a much more appetizing proposition for the hiring manager.

### Pique a Hiring Manager's Interest

You should design your resume in a manner that it will get through applications software, past HR departments and recruiters, and onto a hiring manager's desk or in his / her e-mail in-box, and will then pique their interest. Without that, there will be no interview. Without an interview, you will not get the job you are seeking!

### The Importance of a Resume checklist

_____ Do you have a resume?

_____ Does its very appearance reflect professionalism, competence, organization, etc?

_____ Have you identified accomplishments in your resume?

_____ Are your accomplishments quantifiable?

_____ Is your resume completely clean of typos and grammar difficulties?

_____ Is your resume designed to get past applications software, HR departments and recruiters?

_____ Does your resume present information and elements in a manner that will pique a hiring manager's interest?

# The Mechanics of Resume Writing

*The road to success is always under construction.*
Lily Tomlin

Take a moment and read the quote above by Lily Tomlin…in the mid-1990s I was fortunate enough to attend a conference where Stephen R. Covey, famed inspirational business writer, was speaking. One of the things he said that sunk deeply into my memory banks was this:

> "If you haven't updated your resume in the last six months, you are in trouble."

He went on to make it clear he wasn't talking about the physical revision of your resume, but rather the fact that you needed to be constantly learning and growing, improving your skill set so that you could compete successfully in the world around you.

As you begin writing your resume, there are a number of things you will want to pay particular attention to. Not to do so will affect the value and power of your resume. Elements of your resume you need to pay particular attention to include:

• Acronyms and jargon

- Document types

- Font style

- Formatting

- Hyphens

- Language

- Length

- Look and feel

- Photographs

- Proofreading

Let's take these elements and discuss each briefly:

## Acronyms and Jargon

When writing your resume, you must be cautious with the acronyms and jargon you use. In fact, you should consciously eliminate all acronyms and jargon from your resume to make it more readable and understandable. I will mention this later in the sample resumes chapter, but the resumes of government workers, and especially military workers, are often chock-full of acronyms. But they're not alone – workers from all walks of life and all industries have a tendency to use and over-use acronyms and jargon specific to their corporate culture and their specific company. Doing so often inhibits effective communication between your resume and a potential hiring manager. You must guard against this.

Certain acronyms or jargon might be common to your industry, and a hiring manager will know what you mean. But a human resources person, or a recruiter, may not. Acronyms have their place – it can get unwieldy and awkward – not to mention take up space – to spell out a term every time you use it. If you will be using a term once in your resume, I recommend you spell it out. If you will be using it multiple times, then spell it out the first time, followed by the acronym in parenthesis:

- Senior Professional in Human Resources (SPHR)

- U.S. Pacific Command (USPACOM)

- Electronic Data Interchange (EDI)

- Return on Net Assets (RONA)

- Software as a Service (SAAS)

- Network Operations Center (NOC)

- Business to Business (B2B)

Once you have established the meaning of the acronym, feel free to use it elsewhere in your resume. If you are going to use the acronym in your cover letter, be sure and do the same there too.

By jargon, I mean the terms and vernacular of your current (or most recent) employer. It is often laced with acronyms, which make it that much more difficult to understand. If you have been in the business world long enough – you know what I mean. Each business culture has its own language, its own corporate speak, and sometimes it is difficult to get used to. In one company I worked in, all employees were called associates; in another, associates were non-partner attorneys. An incident from early in my professional career provides an extreme example of cultural jargon: when I began my career, I was in sales for Mountain Bell Telephone. One of my co-workers received a work order (called a bluie by employees because it was on blue paper) indicating that a customer wanted a visit (PV – which stood for Premises Visit) for a business line (a 1FB) on their telephone system (KTS). So, bluie in hand, my co-worker called the customer and said:

> "Hi, this is Rod from Mountain Bell, and I have a bluie here that says you need a PV to discuss getting a 1FB on your KTS."

Understandably, the customer had no idea what my work associate was saying!

**DNUTMA!**

**Do not use too many acronyms**

Jargon and acronyms = a bad combination in resumes and cover letters!

**Document Types**

A special caution on the type document you submit electronically. As of this writing, Word 2007 and Word 2010 are prevalent in the business world. But – they are not pervasive yet. Many companies continue with older versions of Word, and those versions sometimes have difficulty opening Word 2007 / 2010 documents (those that end in .docx). When you send your resume, I would not send it in Word 2007 / 2010; I would use either Word 2003 or even PDF. To do that, you:

- Draft your document in Word 2007 / 2010 as you would normally do;

- If you have already saved it, you'll need to save it again by using the *Save As* command

- When the *Save As* box appears, in the *Save As Type*: window, click on the arrow, and select either *Word 97-2003 document* or *pdf*

- Once you have done that, click on Save and you're done.

When I do that, I usually change the name so I can quickly determine each version from the other: *DQ Resume (old Word)* or *DQ Resume (pdf)*.

I think it is worth the effort to save your resume in a more universal format than run the possibility that your dream job, the one you will get if your resume is reviewed, is offered by a company that has a version of software that can't open .docx files. Don't make your potential hiring manager e-mail you to ask you to resend your documents in a .doc or other format. If you are one of hundreds of applicants, s/he may not (probably won't!) make the effort.

## Font Style

The style of font you use for your resumes is also a critical element not to be taken lightly. I have some personal favorites. For most professional resumes, I prefer Times New Roman or Book Antigua; for IT, engineering and other technical resumes, I still prefer those two fonts, but can live with Arial or Calibri. Generally speaking, I much prefer the former two fonts to the latter two fonts for most resumes. If you use some other font, I am not saying your resume will be rejected, or that you will lose out on the perfect job. What you are going for is a resume that is readable. So – no fancy / ornate fonts.

## Formatting

Formatting is another area you should pay particular attention to on your resume. You want your resume to stand out from the crowd…if it looks like a term paper – devoid of a little bolding and perhaps some judicious italicizing – it may feel flat and uninspiring. Don't go crazy, of course. Consider the difference between the two following resume headings:

Jeffrey L. Blau, Lt. Col. (ret), USMC
Jeff's Address
Jeff's City and Zip Code
Jeff's phone # (h), Jeff's Cell # (c)
Jeff's e-mail address

Summary of Qualifications

and:

# Jeffrey L. Blau, Lt. Col. (ret), USMC
Jeff's Address
Jeff's City and Zip Code
Jeff's phone # (h), Jeff's cell # (c)
Jeff's e-mail address

## SUMMARY OF QUALIFICATIONS

I think you'll agree that the latter resume heading is a little more eye-catching and much more professional looking than the former.

Another important thing to remember when constructing your resume is that many hiring managers are Baby Boomers, and their eyesight is no longer as keen as it used to be. Small font – 8, 10 or 11 – is just too small to read comfortably. Even though I strongly recommend not more than two pages for your resume in most situations, don't sacrifice readability by using small font size. To help you visualize the difference font size makes, here are a few examples in various font sizes (for those Boomers who are reading this, remove your glasses, please!):

**9 and 11 font sizes:**

<u>**Director of Human Resources**</u>                    **August 2001 – August 2011**
Holme Roberts & Owen LLP, Denver, CO

    • Protected the firm from lawsuits by handling all disciplinary actions up to and including terminations using sound employment law practices.  Over the course of ten years and 200+ terminations, there were no lawsuits filed against the firm for employment actions.

**10 and 12 font sizes:**

<u>**Director of Human Resources**</u>                    **August 2001 – August 2011**
Holme Roberts & Owen LLP, Denver, CO

    • Protected the firm from lawsuits by handling all disciplinary actions up to and including terminations using sound employment law practices.  Over the course of ten years and 200+ terminations, there were no lawsuits filed against the firm for employment actions.

**12 and 13 font sizes:**

**<u>Director of Human Resources</u>**                          **August 2001 – August 2011**

Holme Roberts & Owen LLP, Denver, CO

> • Protected the firm from lawsuits by handling all disciplinary actions up to and including terminations using sound employment law practices.  Over the course of ten years and 200+ terminations, there were no lawsuits filed against the firm for employment actions.

Okay, Boomers – you can put your glasses back on….
I think you'll agree the larger font sizes are much more readable than the smaller fonts. You may not believe that some people will try the smaller fonts…but believe it. And after I have been poring over resumes for an hour, those smaller fonts just annoy me!

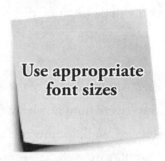

**Length**

Now I will share some counsel that I hope you will listen to…and that is – keep your resume to two pages. If you are just beginning your career, or are only a few years into it, this will be easy. But if you are in the middle of your career, or late in your career, you will find it difficult to limit yourself to two pages.

But try.

If you are a mid- or late-career job seeker, you may ask, "How can I possibly represent my entire career in two pages?" To that question, I have bad news, and I have good news:

• the **bad news** is you probably cannot;

• the **good news** is – you really don't need to.

If you are like me and have been in the business world for 25 to 30+ years, the things you did twenty to thirty years ago have little relevance to the jobs you are seeking today. So don't list them. Concentrate instead on the positions you have held in the past ten to fifteen years. There are several reasons for this:

1. your most recent jobs will (or at least should) have the most relevance to jobs you are currently seeking, and

2. if you list every job you've had since you were a wet-behind-the-ears 18 year old, you will be broadcasting to your potential employer how old you are. And you don't want to do that.

Regarding #2 above, the sad fact is that age discrimination is alive and well. Oh, employers may not be overt about it, but they may do it by reasoning with themselves: "Well, I know this older candidate has more experience, but s/he will cost me $30,000 more in salary to hire them than it will this younger worker who doesn't have as much experience." And of course, there are those who will make the determination based on your age, even though that is illegal. They will never say you are too old…they'll say things like: "You're not a good fit," or "You are over-qualified for this position," or any of a number of other excuses. And that's one of the reasons I am advising you not to list your entire job history.

Not listing your entire work history is the same counsel I provided in *Get a Job!* However, I am willing to be a little flexible on this point. Since *Get a Job!* came out, I have come to understand that many recruiters and employers are beginning to feel like candidates aren't being entirely honest on their resumes if they don't include all their work history. Okay – I can buy that…and I do feel you should always be honest on your resume. But rather than list a ton of other positions that will expand your resume to three pages (or beyond), just put something like:

**Previous Employment History Available Upon Request**

Personally, I am not thrilled about that option, but I could probably live with it. You will have to decide for yourself whether or not you will add that or not. It does, however, broadcast that you are an older worker.

For those of my readers who are younger in their careers, let me add a word about resume length specifically to you: the two-page recommendation is a *maximum* recommendation. If your experience, education and accomplishments don't take your resume to two pages – that is okay! If I am willing to hire someone who doesn't have much experience, I don't expect a two page resume. Perhaps your jobs, experience and education result in a resume that is a page and a half – that's fine. Resist the temptation to add superfluous information to fill the two full pages.

## Hyphens

Because I am obsessive on this issue, may I just say a word or two about hyphens? I shared this information in *Get a Job!*, and even though I have nothing new to add on the topic, it will make me feel better if I can discuss it here.

Even though it probably won't matter too much in your resume since most people don't know how to use hyphens, it will make me feel better.

When two words are used together to modify another word, they should be hyphenated, even if they might not normally be hyphenated. Here's an example:

> The movie was first rate.

> That was a first-rate movie.

In the first sentence, using those two words without a hyphen is just fine. But in the second sentence, the two together form an adjective that modifies the movie – it was a first-rate movie. But wait, in the first sentence we say the movie is first rate – doesn't that phrase modify the movie? Yes, however the rule says you only use the hyphen if it comes before the word.

The exception to this rule is if the first word used ends in –ly:

I was responsible for leading a team of *highly effective* benefits employees.

Since words ending with –ly are actually adverbs, you do not need to use a hyphen with the second word.

Finally, numbers from twenty-one to ninety-nine should be hyphenated (excluding, of course, twenty, thirty, forty, etc.).

As I say, most individuals don't know how to properly use hyphens, so I don't think it will matter if you don't use them correctly in your resume. However, if you are applying for a position as an English teacher, then missing hyphens might be the kiss of death. I always appreciate a candidate whose resume uses hyphens correctly, but I don't consider it a typo when not used.

Thanks. Now I feel better. My wife would tell you that by inserting this section, my OCD is showing. (Except for me, it should be *CDO*, because letters should always be listed in alphabetical order….)

**Photographs**
In case you are tempted, do not include a photograph of yourself with your resume, unless you are seeking an acting or a modeling job. I suppose there may be other career opportunities out there that require a photograph, but the vast majority of jobs in the market don't require it. Even if you are a very attractive individual, most hiring managers and recruiters will simply think it odd that you provided a photograph with your resume.

And besides, if I want to look at your picture, I will look you up on LinkedIn. (So, if you have posted a picture of yourself on LinkedIn, make sure it portrays the professional image you want!)

### Proofreading

An issue you simply cannot be too careful about is the fact that your resume absolutely, positively must be error free when it comes to typos and grammar errors! And – since you will be tailoring your resume to every job for which you apply, you must be ever vigilant that you haven't allowed a typo or two to slip in.

No photos – even if I am pretty!

I am a patient man, generally, and I will usually cut someone a little slack if I run across a typo in their resume; but by the time I hit the second typo, I am about ready to set the resume aside…if I find a third typo, I usually do set it aside (in the "No" pile) and go on to another resume. I had to smile sadly when I found the following strength on a resume I received not too long ago:

  • attenton to detail

(Look at that last bullet point closely…)

Sigh… Every job I know of requires attention to detail (okay, maybe you can blur the lines a bit if you are an impressionistic painter), and typos in a resume are just plain unacceptable to most business people / hiring managers/ recruiters / HR departments.

If you've reviewed as many resumes as I have through the years, you would know there are certain words that are misspelled time and again. Here is my **Top Ten Typos** list:

1. Manger (instead of manager)

2. To (instead of too)

3. Compnay

4. Judgement

5. Responsibile

6. Efficently

7. It's (instead of its)

8. Its (instead of it's)

9. Eht (instead of the)

10. Positon

One of the easiest ways to check your resume for typos is to use your software's spell checker. That will pick up six of the typos listed above. But you also have to be aware of and look for typos (some are more along the lines of incorrect word usage, rather than a typo per se, but I have lumped them together for this discussion) a spell checker won't pick up:

• hear / here

• there / their / they're

• its / it's (learn the difference between these two!)

• affect / effect [if you aren't dead certain when to use these two words, don't use either! (Note: If you don't know the difference between these two words, the effect of the blunder may affect the perception the hiring manager has of your resume!)]

• to / too / two

• stray letters. Did you know that if you leave a letter all by itself in a sentence, spell check doesn't flag it as a spelling error? For example:

The cat n the hat.

Also, watch out for what I call restructuring errors. Word processing software is great and allows you to make rapid revisions. But sometimes, you leave "orphan words" in your sentences. For example:

Original sentence:

> I have been responsible for leading a team of highly effective benefits and payroll employees.

Intended revision:

> I led a team of highly effective benefits and payroll employees.

Final version (with orphans included – **bolding added to highlight the orphans**):

> I **have been** led a team of highly effective benefits and payroll employees.

After you have finished your resume, take the time to read it over with a critical eye. You want to make sure you weed out any and all typos before you send it off. Read it four, five, six times. I am always surprised at errors I pick up on the fifth and sixth readings. I also find it beneficial to start at the last section and work up to the beginning of the resume. When I read it out of order, so to speak, I find that I pick up errors that I might otherwise miss.

Once you have read it over, consider having someone else read it over for you. I have found that spouses, parents and siblings are not good proofreaders – they don't seem to have the critical eye needed to spot errors. Select someone who can find anything you've missed; hopefully your review has been thorough enough that they won't find anything.

One caution – if you ask someone to review your resume, don't be offended by their recommendations. You don't have to incorporate them if you're not comfortable, but don't be offended – they are trying to help you.

I have reviewed resumes and cover letters for years for many people. About ten years ago I met a fellow with whom I went to high school. During the course of our conversation, he shared that he'd been out of work for a while, and was having no success getting interviews at all. When he found out I was in Human Resources, he asked if I would review his resume. Of course I agreed.

To put it bluntly, his resume was a mess. It was no wonder he had not been getting interviews with it. It probably had two dozen typos in it, was poorly formatted, and just wasn't the kind of resume that would be successful in a job hunt. I spent hours revising it – put it into a new format, used some bolding and highlighting, and when I finished, I thought he had a pretty good resume. I sent it off. And heard nothing.

Several months later he contacted me. He told me that when he received his revised resume, he was furious and offended that I would make so many changes. He said that after awhile (a few months), he realized I was just trying to assist him.

Here's one final proofreading hint – if you are like me, you should print your resume and proofread the hard copy. I learned that I am a terrible proofreader on screen. Perhaps you are too.

## The Mechanics of Resume Writing checklist

_____ Watch your use of acronyms and jargon.

_____ Spell out acronyms the first time you use them.

_____ Use judicious formatting.

_____ Make D. Quillen happy – use hyphens correctly.

_____ Except in special circumstances, your resume should be no more than two pages (you can do it!).

_____ Does your resume look crisp and professional?

_____ No photographs!

_____ Proofread effectively.

_____ Make sure you haven't misspelled some of the top misspelled words!

## Key Words and Action Words

*The difference between the right word and the almost right word is the difference between lightning and a lightning bug.*

Mark Twain

As you venture into the job-search world, you will run into any number of individuals whose purpose is to cull your resume out of competition. With hundreds of candidates for many jobs, HR departments and recruiters have that responsibility, as well as applications software. All will be scanning your resume, seeking words that will tell them you have the skills and experience the hiring manager is seeking – or not. They will be looking for key words which are relevant to the open position. If they find them, you may move to the next level of consideration; if not, then you can expect a "Thank you, but no thank you," e-mail or letter. You would be well advised to tailor your resume to each job for which you are applying, using the key words that hiring managers have identified as critical to their open job. Let's discuss where you might find key words.

**Job ads** are a great – and crucial -- source for key words. They tell you what the language is at the company that has the job opening, and the key words included in their job ad are what their people and their applications software will be looking for when they screen resumes. Are they looking for someone skilled in evaluations? Then use the term evaluations in your resume, not performance management. If they use Business-to-Business and you use B2B, your resume may get screened out, because the software wasn't looking for B2B. And can you be certain they will be searching for the term CRM, or will they spell it out: Customer Relationship Management?

Following is an actual job ad for a programmer, with the key words bolded:

## Programmer

### About the Job

Direct client has a need for an **Applications Programmer** for a 12-month contract position:

The Product Service Team within the Applications organization is in need of a **programmer senior** - specifically to work on the **Special Lines Internet Quoting (SLIQ)** application. The SLIQ application is written on a **proprietary framework** which utilizes **XML** to generate the **user interfaces** and **navigational flows**. The ideal candidate will have experience with **CSS**, **HTML** and **XML**. Training or experience with **C#.Net** would be a plus – but not required. Also, prior experience with **TFS** would be beneficial but not required.

There are several projects to enhance the SLIQ application. Some projects are already defined while others are in process of **documenting requirements** and being estimated. These projects will range in total hours from 250 - 1000 and we may choose to bundle multiple projects into a larger project with a PM and project team. The ideal candidate will have the ability to work within a dynamic environment with the ability to handle multiple projects when required.

**Required Skills:**

• **HTML**

• **XML**

• **CSS**

• Training or experience with **C#. NET** is a plus, but not required.

• Prior experience with **TFS** would be beneficial but not required

• Experience working with **proprietary frameworks** is a plus and **good communication, interpersonal skills**, and a **self-starter**.

**Job descriptions** are also a good place to look for key words, words you will want to use in your resume to catch the attention of those who are screening your resume. You can find job descriptions on the Internet by Googling _____ (specific job) job description. Following is an example of a sample job description I got by typing *Programmer job description*:

> **Programmer Job Purpose**: **Creates** and **modifies** computer programs by converting **project requirements** into **code**.
>
> **Programmer Job Duties**:
>
> • Confirms project requirements by reviewing **program objective**, **input data**, and **output requirements** with analyst, supervisor, and client.
>
> • Arranges project requirements in **programming sequence** by **analyzing requirements**; preparing a **work flow chart** and **diagram** using knowledge of computer capabilities, subject matter, **programming language**, and **logic**.
>
> • **Encodes** project requirements by converting **work flow information** into **computer language**.
>
> • **Programs** the computer by entering **coded information**.
>
> • Confirms program operation by **conducting tests**; **modifying program sequence** and/or codes.
>
> • Prepares reference for users by writing **operating instructions**.

• Maintains historical records by documenting **program development** and **revisions**.

• Maintains client confidence and protects operations by keeping information confidential.

• Ensures operation of equipment by following manufacturer's instructions; **troubleshooting malfunctions**; calling for repairs; **evaluating new equipment** and techniques.

• Maintains professional and technical knowledge by attending educational workshops; reviewing professional publications; establishing personal networks; participating in professional societies.

• Contributes to team effort by accomplishing related results as needed.

• **Skills/Qualifications: General Programming Skills, Analyzing Information, Problem Solving, Software Algorithm Design, Software Performance Tuning, Attention to Detail, Software Design, Software Debugging, Software Development Fundamentals, Software Documentation, Software Testing**

As with the actual job ad, I have **bolded** a number of key words from this job description. The nice thing about searching for key words in generic job descriptions is that you will often find a lot of key industry-specific words that can be used in your resume. The downside is that those key words may not be specific to the job for which you are applying; in fact, job descriptions are pretty general, and will lack the specificity of what you will find in job ads.

Speaking of specificity, compare the key words identified in the generic job description with those in the actual job ad just before it. If you were a programmer with the skills and experience that was being sought in the actual job ad, you would be much better served – and more likely to get an interview -- by using the key words from the job ad in your resume than if you create a resume using the less-specific key words from the generic job description.

**Recruiters** are also good sources of hot key words. If you are working with a recruiter, visit with them about your resume and have them weigh in on whether or not you have the right key words in it. They will likely help you revise your resume toward specific job openings they have.

**Job Boards** are also great places to seek key words. Not only will you find job ads there, but you can see what key words come up repeatedly in various jobs. Each week, one job board – The Ladders – updates their list of the Top 100 key words searched by recruiters. You can find their latest list at *www.theladders.com/career-advice/top-100-resume-keywords/*. At the time of this writing, the top twenty key words recruiters had been searching for were:

1.  Sales

2.  Tax

3.  Marketing

4.  Software Sales

5.  Healthcare

6.  Insurance

7.  Manufacturing

8.  Retail

9.  Medical device

10. Sales Manager

11. Financial Advisor

12. Medical

13. SAP

14. Medical Sales

15. Audit

16. Food

17. Recruiter

18. Construction

19. Project manager

20. Software sales manager

## KEY WORDS AND ACTION WORDS

In addition to key words, a way to craft your resume so that it captures the attention of screeners is to use action words to describe your responsibilities and activities. Nothing new here – I have been hearing about action / power words for several decades now. These words can help spice up your resume a bit. Some typical ones include:

- Accelerated

- Assessed

- Coached

- Coded

- Collaborated

- Created

- Conceived

- Delegated

- Designed

- Developed

- Devised

- Directed

- Enabled

- Enhanced

- Enriched

- Established

- Evaluated

- Fashioned

- Financed

- Guided

- Initiated

- Instituted

- Integrated

- Interpreted

- Mentored

- Negotiated

- Prioritized

- Promoted

- Publicized

- Recommended

And if those aren't enough to get you started, just Google *Resume power words* and you'll receive an avalanche of websites that will help you find words that will perk up and strengthen your resume. One of my favorite websites for this is at Careerealism: *www.careerealism.com/top-resume-words/*.

So – take a look and see if you can't find a word or two that will assist you in strengthening your resume.

# KEY WORDS AND ACTION WORDS

**Key Words and Action Words checklist**

_____ It is important to use key words in your resume.

_____ You can find key words in job ads, job descriptions, on the Internet.

_____ Use action / power words to spice up your resume language.

_____ Check the Internet and other sources for action words.

# List Your Accomplishments!

*Being busy does not always mean real work. The object of all work is production or accomplishment and to either of these ends there must be forethought, system, planning, intelligence, and honest purpose, as well as perspiration. Seeming to do is not doing.*
Thomas Edison

A resume without accomplishments is like bacon without eggs, peanut butter without jelly, yin without yang – it just shouldn't be done!

I have to tell you – most of the resumes I review are seriously devoid of **accomplishments**. They are often filled with *tasks* – things the person *did* – but lacking anything that identifies how well they did those tasks, or what difference those tasks made – no accomplishments. There is nothing to differentiate the candidate from the many other candidates applying for the same job.

As a hiring manager, I am always interested in accomplishments – not only do I want to know *what* a candidate did, I want to know *how well* they did it. Here is an entry from a resume I recently reviewed:

> • Responsible for developing office budgets and addressing concerns and issues as they arose.

My problem with that statement isn't that this candidate was responsible for something…I want to know how well they have discharged that responsibility? Here's the same entry, with an accomplishment that tells how well this person did in that responsibility:

Show HOW I did my job, not just WHAT I did

- Responsible for developing office budgets and addressing concerns and issues as they arose. **In ten years as office manager, never came in over budget, even though several difficult situations arose that required creative and budget-conscious problem solving.**

Ah – an office manager who was budget conscious, always came in under budget, but was still flexible enough to figure out solutions to difficult issues that arose, and did so within the constraints of her budget. You may be saying, "So what?" I'll tell you what the "So what?" is – as a hiring manager, I am much more likely to call this person in for an interview than to call the person who doesn't tell me how well he or she did their job.

The evening before I wrote this chapter, I received a resume from a friend -- Mark. He had lost his job and as part of his networking effort, shared his resume with me. Among other things, his resume contained the following items:

**Product Roadmap Manager (June 2013 – Present)**
- Maintained the company-wide product roadmap and managed overall demand capacity for six Agile project teams.

  ¶ Increased productivity by 44% – Agile teams better understood resource consumption and utilization.

- Metrics-driven; weekly in-depth analysis of development stream, in concert with the Release Manager, greatly enhanced all operational elements – improved product quality (reduced production defects by 32%).

• Supported successful launch of two product enhancements -- enabled greater user self configurability and reduced internal on-going implementation and maintenance costs by over $2.5 million annually.

• Partnered with Customer Success Organization; client software enhancement response time reduced from six months to three weeks, enhanced clients relations, added predictability to processes, and increased development stream velocity.

• Crafted first-ever scope change addition/request templates; created ability to better track and document scope changes after scope freeze date -- led to a deeper understanding of scope changes and communicated to senior leaders what risk is being introduced into a release.

So – did you pick up on the accomplishments he included in his list of tasks? Here is the list of his responsibilities again, but this time I have **highlighted** his accomplishments in bold:

**Product Roadmap Manager (June 2013 – Present)**

• Maintained the company-wide product roadmap and managed overall demand capacity for six Agile project teams.

**¶ Increased productivity by 44% – Agile teams better understood resource consumption and utilization.**

• Metrics-driven; weekly in-depth analysis of development stream, in concert with the Release Manager, **greatly enhanced all operational elements – improved product quality (reduced production defects by 32%).**

• Supported successful launch of two product enhancements – **enabled greater user self configurability and reduced internal on-going implementation and maintenance costs by over $2.5 million annually.**

# LIST YOUR ACCOMPLISHMENTS

• Partnered with Customer Success Organization; **client software enhancement response time reduced from six months to three weeks, enhanced clients relations, added predictability to processes**, and **increased development stream velocity**.

• Crafted **first-ever** scope change addition/request templates; **created ability to better track and document scope changes after scope freeze date – led to a deeper understanding of scope changes** and **communicated to senior leaders what risk is being introduced into a release**.

Here is a summary of the accomplishments my friend Mark provided for his responsibilities:

1. **Increased productivity by 44%.**

2. **Agile teams better understood resource consumption and utilization.**

3. **Greatly enhanced all operational elements.**

4. **Improved product quality (reduced production defects by 32%).**

5. **Enabled greater user self configurability.**

6. **Reduced internal on-going implementation and maintenance costs by over $2.5 million annually.**

7. **Client software enhancement response time reduced from six months to three weeks.**

8. **Enhanced client relations.**

9. **Added predictability to processes.**

10. **Increased development stream velocity.**

11. **Crafted first-ever scope change addition/request templates.**

12. **Created ability to better track and document scope changes after scope freeze date.**

13. **Led to a deeper understanding of scope changes.**

14. **Communicated to senior leaders what risk is being introduced into a release.**

So in the six responsibilities / tasks he listed, Mark was able to list fourteen accomplishments! Had he not included those accomplishments, here is what his resume entries would have looked like:

**Product Roadmap Manager (June 2013 – Present)**

    • Maintained the company-wide product roadmap and managed overall demand capacity for six Agile project teams.

    • Metrics-driven; weekly in-depth analysis of development stream.

    • Supported successful launch of two product enhancements.

    • Partnered with Customer Success Organization.

    • Crafted scope change addition/request templates;

I leave it to you, dear reader – which of those entries piques your interest more – the one with the accomplishment statements, or the one without? I can tell you which one interests me more as a hiring manager – the one that told me how well Mark did his job!

As you scan the list of Mark's accomplishments, you'll note the accomplishments he lists fall into two categories – quantifiable and non-quantifiable (soft) accomplishments. Let me discuss both categories of accomplishments briefly:

**Quantifiable Accomplishments**

The quantifiable accomplishments Mark listed were:

1. **Increased productivity by 44%.**

2. **Improved product quality (reduced production defects by 32%).**

3. **Client software enhancement response time reduced from six months to three weeks.**

4. **Reduced internal on-going implementation and maintenance costs by over $2.5 million annually.**

Those are great accomplishments – they show that Mark's leadership and abilities made a positive impact to the bottom line of his company. Quantifiable accomplishments are of course the best accomplishments to include in your resume.

### Non-Quantifiable (Soft) Accomplishments

While quantifiable accomplishments are preferred whenever you can identify them, sometimes things simply can't be quantified. But when that's the case, don't give up, and certainly don't ignore them. Even though non-quantifiable, it is better to add these accomplishments than leave them out. Looking over Mark's entries again, here are his non-quantifiable accomplishments:

1. **Agile teams better understood resource consumption and utilization.**

2. **Greatly enhanced all operational elements.**

3. **Enabled greater user self configurability.**

4. **Enhanced client relations.**

5. **Added predictability to processes.**

6. **Increased development stream velocity.**

7. **Crafted first-ever scope change addition/request templates.**

8. **Created ability to better track and document scope changes after scope freeze date.**

9. **Led to a deeper understanding of scope changes.**

10. **Communicated to senior leaders what risk is being introduced into a release.**

As you scan those accomplishments, I think you'll agree that some are difficult to quantify – enhancing client relations, adding predictability to processes, deeper understanding of changes, etc. But providing them is better than leaving the task alone, unsupported by successes.

Before we go a step further, I suspect you already have a resume. Pull it out – in a moment we'll have you take a little *accomplishments* test…We'll review your resume as it exists today, and assign a score – like you received on tests when you were in school – to your resume.

Before we apply this test to your resume, let me provide a couple actual entries from several resumes, and let's see how those candidates did in placing accomplishments in their resumes. The first resume was one I reviewed for a friend not long ago; the second example is from my resume.

Below are ten entries from the resume of a Benefits Account Executive. I have put a check mark in front of each entry that has an accomplishment associated with it; I have also **bolded** those accomplishments:

✓ _____ Received **highest** retention award for 2012 **(100% retention)**

_____ Develop and implement retention strategies for a block of large self-funded and fully insured health plans.

_____ Provide consultative services to clients on plan design, alternative financial arrangements and innovative plan management opportunities.

_____ Extensive experience in both self-funded and fully insured financial arrangements. (Minimum Premium, Administrative Services Only, as well as stop loss contracts).

_____ Served as representative on Federal Employee Program (FEP); responsible for 10 counties.

_____ On an annual basis, analyzed and determined premium, expense and risk levels for all assigned cases.

_____ Prepared analysis by compiling claims information of benefit utilization.

_____ Determined cost and risk factors for proposed funding or benefits.

_____ Assisted in negotiation with brokers or policy holders and helped educate the field representatives on products and procedures.

✓ _____ **Promoted four times** during tenure.

# LIST YOUR ACCOMPLISHMENTS

So my friend had ten entries, and only two accomplishments – a score of 20% -- no gold stars for him!

Here's another quick example, this time from my resume as a Director of HR:

✓____ Protected the firm from lawsuits by handling all disciplinary actions up to and including terminations using sound employment law practices. **Over the course of ten years and 200+ terminations, there were no lawsuits filed against the firm for employment actions**.

✓✓ Effectively managed all health benefits for the firm. Over a five-year period, **negotiated over $2,000,000 in savings for the firm while maintaining one of the best benefits packages in our market (excellent benefits, low deductibles, moderate premiums, etc.)**.

✓____ Skilled at cultural transformation and organizational design. Over the past ten years, several firm mergers / acquisitions required effective cultural assimilation and organizational design. **Efforts resulted in rapid employee and partner assimilation and a more efficient work force**.

✓✓ As part of an employee engagement and retention effort, developed, launched and administered a voluntary staff development program designed to enhance staff skills, improve client service and enrich the work experience for employees. **Ongoing classes supported and attended by over 90% of staff. Hailed as a significant success by firm management**.

✓____ Used competency modeling expertise to assess required skills for positions, and identified skill gaps within the work force. Training curricula developed to address deficiencies within the various work groups, **resulting in a more efficient and skilled work force**.

✓____ When the Director of Legal Recruiting left the firm, was asked to take over those responsibilities while maintaining Director of HR responsibilities. **Served in dual roles for eighteen months, saving the firm over $250,000 in salary expense**.

✓____ **Due to success in complex HR situations**, was asked to provide HR support to 1,400 Avaya Labs (formerly Bell Labs) scientists, a large department with significant complexity to their HR work. **Earned *Exceeded* and *Far Exceeded* ratings and performance bonuses for work with this group**.

✓ Designed a recruiting strategy for our business unit, aimed at recruiting and selecting only "A" players into our business. Allowed the company to bring in more qualified employees, reducing turnover and increasing productivity. **Business unit strategy was so successful it served as a model for corporate-wide recruiting**.

✓ Designed and implemented an organization-wide learning curriculum for managers. Resulting programs identified competency gaps and provided customized learning curricula for managers. **Efforts hailed by company executives as break-through, creative and highly efficient**.

✓ Certified as a Competency Consultant. **Because of success in this area**, was asked to work with a small team to introduce competency modeling company-wide, including international locations. Competency modeling used for recruiting, employee development and performance management.

So, for my ten entries, I actually had twelve accomplishments – 120% -- I always liked getting extra credit when I was in school.

Now it's your turn – let's see how your current resume scores on such an accomplishments review. Following are a few steps to help you do this:

**Resume Accomplishments Test**

Locate your resume and print it.

1.  Now, write the first ten responsibility and task entries from your resume onto the following lines:

    1. _____

    2. _____

    3. _____

# LIST YOUR ACCOMPLISHMENTS

4. _____

5. _____

6. _____

7. _____

8. _____

9. _____

10. _____

2. Now – write down all the accomplishment statements you have in the first ten entries for your tasks and responsibilities:

1. _____

2. _____

3. _____

4. _____

5. _____

6. _____

7. _____

8. _____

9. _____

10. _____

3. Look at your entries and your **accomplishments**, and determine your score:

   a. Write the score at the top of your resume (9 accomplishments = 90%, 8 accomplishments = 80%, etc.)

b.   Now, if your score is:

    i.   90% or better, you are doing well – better than most – in identifying accomplishments;

    ii.   Between 80% and 89%, you're near the top of the class – can you add one or two more?

    iii.   Between 70% and 79%, you're definitely on the right track, but you can strengthen your resume with a few more accomplishments.

    iv.   Below 70%, you really need to put some concentrated focus into this effort. A little time and energy now will pay dividends later.

I understand how difficult identifying and listing accomplishments can be. Here's what works for me: As I read an entry on my resume, I ask myself,

"What can I say about this activity / task / responsibility that will show my potential boss that I performed it well?"

I understand some tasks will be difficult to differentiate your performance, but you must try.

For a little accomplishments practice, let's refer back to the first example in this chapter. Let's see if we can come up with a few more accomplishments for the Benefits Account Executive's resume we reviewed earlier. I am not a Benefits Account Executive, but I have had them call on me frequently and support me through the years of my tenure as a Director of HR. So I know a little about their work.

Below is the list of tasks / activities again; at the end of each activity I have **added** a potential accomplishment:

✔   **Received highest retention award for 2012 (100% retention).**

# LIST YOUR ACCOMPLISHMENTS

✓ Develop and implement retention strategies for a block of large self-funded and fully insured health plans. **Strategies were successful – all clients were retained going into 2013**.

✓ Provide consultative services to clients on plan design, alternative financial arrangements and innovative plan management opportunities. **Consultation allowed clients to make sensible plan changes that lessened the impact of premium increases. Support and consultation enhanced client relations**.

✓ Extensive experience in both self-funded and fully insured financial arrangements. (Minimum Premium, Administrative Services Only, as well as stop loss contracts). **Was able to use this experience to satisfy the benefits and funding needs of clients as evidenced by retention of all clients**.

_____ Served as representative on Federal Employee Program (FEP); responsible for 10 counties.

✓ On an annual basis, analyzed and determined premium, expense and risk levels for all assigned cases. **Analysis praised by account teams and protected the company's assets. Was able to help clients understand the reason for premium increases, and opened the way for additional discussions on plan changes, wellness initiatives, etc**.

✓ Prepared analysis by compiling claims information of benefit utilization. **Analyses always followed an understandable and logical format, allowing account teams and clients to easily understand the information being provided.**

✓ Determined cost and risk factors for proposed funding or benefits. **Analysis struck a balance between protecting the company and retaining the customer**.

✓ Assisted in negotiation with brokers or policy holders and helped educate the field representatives on products and procedures. **Underwriting expertise allowed discussion to be informative, accurate and productive, helping**

**clients understand the reason for premium increases, and helping clients adjust plans to lessen impact of poor claims experience.**

✓ **Promoted four times during tenure.**

How did we do? From a list of activities that initially only offered 20% accomplishments, we're now at 90%. The goal of this exercise is to show the hiring manager we can be a valuable contributor to their company.

**Still Not Convinced?**

What's that you say? You didn't know you needed accomplishments on your resume? Or perhaps you have heard that before, but, well, it sure seems like a lot of work to identify accomplishments.

Yes it is a lot of work to identify accomplishments, but you want to do all you can to convince the recruiter, HR department or hiring manager that you are great at what you do – not just some mediocre employee out there going through the paces. Let's revise an entry from my resume listed above, removing the accomplishment statements:

> • Provided support to 1,400 Avaya Labs (formerly Bell Labs) scientists, a large department with significant complexity to their HR work.

So I supported a department of 1,400 Avaya Labs employees. So what?! Maybe I was the worst HR person they'd ever had! That seems pretty typical of the kinds of entries I see on many (most) resumes. In fact, it's a lot like most of the entries for the Benefits Account Executive we reviewed earlier. Now let's look at my entry again, this time with the accomplishments included:

> • **Due to success in complex HR situations,** was asked to provide HR support to 1,400 Avaya Labs (formerly Bell Labs) scientists, a large department with significant complexity to their HR work. **Earned *Exceeded* and *Far Exceeded* ratings and performance bonuses for work with this group.**

# LIST YOUR ACCOMPLISHMENTS

So, these two accomplishment statements tell the hiring manager that I did a good job on the tasks and responsibilities assigned to me:

- **Due to success in complex HR situations**, and

- **Earned *Exceeded* and *Far Exceeded* ratings and performance bonuses for work with this group**.

Some accomplishments are relatively easy to determine:

- Achieved 127% of annual sales quota;

- Developed and led an expense-reduction project that saved the company $1,250,000 over a two-year period;

- Surveys demonstrated positive public opinion increased 18% over a six-month period as a result of Public Affairs outreach campaign.

Working as an HR professional for twenty-plus years, I understand sometimes it is difficult to quantify accomplishments. But you still must try. It's worth the effort -- it's okay if some of your accomplishments are a little soft (i.e. -- not quantifiable), but you should strive to have an accomplishment for every entry you have on your resume. And here's a hint – if you can't think of an accomplishment…is the task / activity important enough to be included in your resume?

Okay – so these are really easy if you are a top performer, and if you have met and exceeded your goals and objectives. But what if you haven't? What if you have fallen short of expectations? Let's say you're a sales representative who missed your sales objective for two years in a row – what do you do then?

Well – you look for the best possible way to represent your time in that job. Let's say you joined your company as a sales rep and they gave you the territory that had been the dog for years – no sales rep had been successful with it. You were doomed to failure before you began. And indeed, after two years, you were still able to only muster hitting 72% and 80% of your target. If that's the case, then perhaps here's your resume entry:

**Accentuate the positive – add accomplishments**

- Assigned one of the company's historically most difficult sales territories. Through diligent effort and perseverance, was able to produce 50% more from this territory than any previous sales rep.

- Increased sales 11% year-over-year in a traditionally difficult territory.

Look for and accentuate the positive in all your resume entries.

Maybe you didn't succeed – maybe you took that difficult territory and performed about the same as all your predecessors did – miserably. What were the positives? Did you re-establish relationships with former clients who had become disgruntled with your company? Even if they didn't buy from you, include that. Did you identify and bring new clients in? Tell us about it.

Remember – you want to stand out as a candidate for the hiring manager…and I guarantee that if you are able to add accomplishments to your resume – even soft ones – that will make you stand out from many / most of the candidates who are applying for the same job as you.

### Accomplishments checklist

_____ Did you review your resume, looking for accomplishments?

_____ What percentage of your resume entries had accomplishments?

_____ If fewer than 80% of your entries have accomplishments, try to identify and include accomplishments for at least 80% of your entries.

_____ For those entries that don't have accomplishments, can you think of one?

_____ If you cannot think of an accomplishment for an entry, should the entry be in your resume? Is there a different entry – with an accomplishment -- that will better showcase your talents and capabilities?

# LIST YOUR ACCOMPLISHMENTS

_____ Did all your entries (tasks / responsibilities) have an accomplishment included?

_____ Did you accentuate the positive, even though you may have fallen short of expectations?

_____ Does your resume tell the hiring manager that you are successful at what you do?

_____ Do **not** ignore this chapter!

# Appearance Matters

*With me it's always about first impressions.*
Billy Zane

When you go to a job interview, you have one chance to make a good first impression. Before you say a word, your potential employer is already sizing you up -- drawing his or her conclusions about you – and how you are dressed sends a powerful message. Are you dressed professionally, or are you dressed too casually for the position and/or the culture of the company? Is your clothing crisp and clean, or wrinkled and worn out? Do you project a professional image, or not? Sharp or dull? Poised or nervous?

*And so it is with your resume.* As short as it may seem, it takes me 3 to 5 seconds to determine whether or not I am interested in the candidate represented by the resume…and part of that 3 to 5 seconds is what I think about the look and feel of the resume.

When I look at a resume, my first thoughts – whether conscious or unconscious – are about what it looks like. I notice whether it feels cramped, whether it's too cluttered. I notice whether it looks professional, or whether it looks amateurish. Cursed with a proofreader's eye, typos and grammar difficulties leap off the page at me. I notice whether the resume is sharp – or dull.

Literally on the day I was writing this chapter, I received a resume from the friend of a friend. My friend had told her friend about my previous book, *Get a Job!*, and assured him I would be able to give him some pointers about his resume.

The resume arrived attached in an e-mail. I opened his resume and glanced at it. My first thought was…vanilla. With a few minor edits (name, address, etc.), following is the resume, as it arrived in my inbox. The real name, of course, has been changed to protect the innocent!

---

Weston Good Guy
Weston's Street Address
Weston's city, state, & zip code
Weston's telephone #
WestonGoodGuy@xxx.com

<u>Summary</u>

A problem solver that has over 12 years of case management success and success with research and analysis experience. Supervised staff and work crews as a result delivered a proven track record of exceeding expectations, delivery, and quality work.

Manager. Interpersonal Skills. Professional. Human Resources. Communicator. Facilitation. Data Collection. Research. Interviewer. Conflict Resolution. Statistical Analysis. Trainer. Mediation. Contract Negotiation.

<u>Professional Experience</u>

<u>CPS Specialist II (Case Manager II)</u>

State of Arizona, Department of Economic Security, Child Protective Services
2011-2013

- Educating clients through the process of State services, assessing child safety and risk through face-to-face contact, finding related programs for clients for successful problem resolution and negotiation.

---

- Primary point of contact for clients and interfacing with departmental staff to meet project marketing requirements.

- Conferring with attorneys and participating in exhibits and discovery responses for court hearings which lead to successful family unity and efficient contract coordination while maintaining confidentiality.

- Preparing review of testimony and conducting case plan staffing which proceeded in the successful delivery of professional reports and documents for statistical analysis and research as well as data collection while being proficient at Microsoft Office, Outlook, Word, and Excel.

- Development of basic analytical and technical capabilities in order to meet established goals in a timely and professional manner.

-Maintain a Level One Fingerprint Clearance Card through the Department of Public Safety

Supervisor

City of Broken Arrow OK, Broken Arrow Police Department     2003-2011

-  Efficient case management by keeping up to date daily, weekly, and monthly analysis of crime statistics for direct communication to city prosecutors and circuit court Judges.

- Responsible for the direct supervision management of up to 8 staff including hiring, training, reviewing, and discipline.

- Help develop a 12 hour schedule for the jail staff that saved the City over $36,000 in annual overtime.

- Conducted cost studies and other analysis to meet regulatory requirements. Training and seminars on various techniques and legal topics for new and existing staff in order to stay accredited by jail standards for the State of Oklahoma and the Federal Government.

- Maintaining relationship management and booking of inmates and keeping safety within the separate pods of inmates and prisoners.

- Received a commendation from the Chief of Police for my involvement in the departmental Leadership Team.

<u>Supervisor</u>

USIC Utility Company
1998 – 2002

- Entry level position where I attained a position to management levels, ultimately managing a successful team of 18 crew members.

- Lead the team in underground utility plant protection in a timely, accurate, and safe manner.

- Constant communication with various construction foremen to go over blueprints and read underground maps for various utilities that needed protection in a stressful atmosphere.

- Proactively negotiated contracts with clients in a direct manner for business success and deliver quality to the client.

- Was able to save company costs by 30% by efficiently maintaining crew locations and labor wage percentages.

<u>Education</u>

Bachelor's Degree                                        University of Oklahoma

Master's Degree - Master of Business Administration (Comp 2015) Grand Canyon University

<u>Professional Training</u>

Case Management Training of 278 hours: State Sponsored

Police Executive Decision And Leadership class, University of Tulsa: Police Sponsored

As I said – vanilla. Boring. Uninspiring. Flat.

Aside from underlining a few entries, he used no formatting. Basically, his resume just lays there, begging to be consigned to the "No, thanks," pile.

I asked him if I could spice it up a little bit, and he agreed. After a little tinkering, with some formatting here and some different fonts there, the resume you see on the next two pages is what I came up with. I have made no changes at all to the content...

# WESTON G. GUY

Street Address, City, State & Zip Code     303-555-1212     WestonGoodGuy@xxx.com

## SUMMARY

A problem solver that has over 12 years of case management success and success with research and analysis experience. Supervised staff and work crews as a result delivered a proven track record of exceeding expectations, delivery, and quality work. Interpersonal Skills

- Professional
- Human Resources
- Communicator
- Facilitation

- Data Collection
- Research
- Interviewer
- Conflict Resolution

- Statistical Analysis
- Trainer
- Mediation
- Contract Negotiation

## PROFESSIONAL EXPERIENCE

**CPS Specialist II (Case Manager II)**                    **2011 to 2013**
State of Arizona, Department of Economic Security, Child Protective Services

- Educating clients through the process of State services, assessing child safety and risk through face-to-face contact, finding related programs for clients for successful problem resolution and negotiation.
- Primary point of contact for clients and interfacing with departmental staff to meet project marketing requirements.
- Conferring with attorneys and participating in exhibits and discovery responses for court hearings which lead to successful family unity and efficient contract coordination while maintaining confidentiality.
- Preparing review of testimony and conducting case plan staffing which proceeded in the successful delivery of professional reports and documents for statistical analysis and research as well as data collection while being proficient at Microsoft Office, Outlook, Word, and Excel.
- Development of basic analytical and technical capabilities in order to meet established goals in a timely and professional manner.
- Maintain a Level One Fingerprint Clearance Card through the Department of Public Safety.

**Supervisor**                    **2003 to 2011**
City of Broken Arrow OK, Broken Arrow Police Department

- Efficient case management by keeping up to date daily, weekly, and monthly analysis of crime statistics for direct communication to city prosecutors and circuit court Judges.
- Responsible for the direct supervision and management of up to 8 staff including hiring, training, reviewing, and discipline.
- Help develop a 12 hour schedule for the jail staff that saved the City over $36,000 in annual overtime.
- Conducted cost studies and other analysis to meet regulatory requirements. Training and seminars on various techniques and legal topics for new and existing staff in order to stay accredited by jail standards for the State of Oklahoma and the Federal Government.
- Maintaining relationship management and booking of inmates and keeping safety within the separate pods of inmates and prisoners.
- Received a commendation from the Chief of Police for my involvement in the departmental Leadership Team.

**Supervisor**                                                                          **1998 to 2002**
USIC Utility Company

- Entry level position where I attained a position to management levels, ultimately managing a successful team of 18 crew members.
- Lead the team in underground utility plant protection in a timely, accurate, and safe manner.
- Constant communication with various construction foremen to go over blueprints and read underground maps for various utilities that needed protection in a stressful atmosphere.
- Proactively negotiated contracts with clients in a direct manner for business success and deliver quality to the client.
- Was able to save company costs by 30% by efficiently maintaining crew locations and labor wage percentages.

## EDUCATION

**Bachelor's Degree**                                                    **University of Oklahoma**

**Master's Degree - Master of Business Administration (Comp 2015) Grand Canyon University**

## PROFESSIONAL TRAINING

**Case Management Training** of 278 hours: State Sponsored

**Police Executive Decision and Leadership** class, University of Tulsa: Police Sponsored

# APPEARANCE MATTERS

With exactly the same content, I think you will agree that if you saw both of these resumes resting side-by-side on a desk (or sitting in a stack of resumes), the second resume just *looks* more professional. The look and feel of your resume is important – even before you get to the content. If the hiring manager is underwhelmed or worse yet -- turned off -- by the appearance of your resume, then you run the risk of your job search ending abruptly without a word of the content being read. That sounds harsh (and it is a bit), but it is the truth.

**Margins** are important in resumes. If you have taken to heart my counsel to limit your resume to two pages – good for you! However, if to do so you have filled it with text from top to bottom and left to right by cutting down the margins of the resume to their barest minimums, then that's not what I am suggesting. Your resume should look clean, and that can be accomplished by having good white space – adequate borders (top, bottom, left, right), appropriate space between lines and paragraphs. Not to do this makes your resume feel cramped, and lowers its visual appeal.

While it is important to spice up your resume, please don't go overboard. Don't choose to spice it up with some out-of-the-ordinary font, don't add color, and unless you are looking for a job as an actor or actress, don't include your photograph!

Keep it clean, sharp and professional.

**A note**: while the **format** of Weston's resume looks more professional, there is still a LOT of work that needs to be done to make it stronger: better word flow, stronger words, more accomplishments, etc. The example above was just to help you see the difference a little formatting can make in the appearance of a resume.

### Appearance Matters checklist

_____ What message does your resume send just laying there? Professional or amateurish? Sharp or dull? Cramped? Interesting or not?

_____ Is there plenty of white space – top, bottom and side margins?

_____ Does your resume feel flat, vanilla?

## THE PERFECT RESUME

_____ Could your resume be spruced up a bit by adding judicious formatting?

_____ Is your resume completely clean of typos and grammar difficulties?

## Resume Language

*If you talk to a man in a language he understands, that goes to his head. If you talk to him in his language, that goes to his heart.*
Nelson Mandela

The language you use in your resume is important. While I am sure that last sentence makes sense to you, it really is true. The language you use in your resume helps set the stage for your professional presentation.

At the beginning of my career, I met with my boss to receive my first-ever performance review. I remember exactly two things from that meeting: the first isn't relevant to our discussion here, but the second is very relevant. My boss told me that my writing was too informal, and that I needed to strive to be a little more formal in my writing.

That seemed like good advice at the time, and I think it is good advice when you are putting your resume together. Don't be too informal in your resume language and presentation.

Most resumes use what I call **Resume Shorthand**; it uses sentences, but sort of… abbreviated. Pronouns – such as I, me, we, our, etc., are seldom used. Some have observed that their use in resumes shows an amateurish streak. I am not particularly bothered about that, but I do know that most resumes I review don't use pronouns. Here are a few examples of resume entries, first in proper English, next in resume shorthand:

**Proper English**

> • When the Director of Legal Recruiting left our firm, I was asked to take over her responsibilities while maintaining my Director of HR responsibilities. I served in dual roles for eighteen months, saving the firm over $250,000 in salary expense.

**Resume Shorthand**

> • When the Director of Legal Recruiting left the firm, was asked to take over those responsibilities while maintaining Director of HR responsibilities. Served in dual roles for eighteen months, saving the firm over $250,000 in salary expense.

**Proper English**

> • I was responsible for supporting the planning and execution of USPACOM exercises throughout the Asia Pacific region. I was asked to facilitate small group, focused problem-solving discussions by senior civilian and military leaders of allied and partner nations.

**Resume Shorthand**

> • Supported the planning / execution of USPACOM exercises throughout the Asia Pacific region. Facilitated small group, focused problem-solving discussions by senior civilian and military leaders of allied and partner nations.

**Proper English**

> • I minimized the erosion of the firm's receivables through implementation of more stringent business processes.

**Resume Shorthand**

> • Minimized erosion of firm's receivables through implementation of more stringent business processes.

# RESUME LANGUAGE

**Proper English**

• I was responsible for managing the Employment & Compensation, Benefits, Talent Acquisition and Training teams for the City of Aurora, Colorado.

**Resume Shorthand**

• Managed Employment & Compensation, Benefits, Talent Acquisition and Training teams for the City of Aurora, Colorado.

It may not seem like this makes a big difference, but it does. You should become adept in and comfortable with resume shorthand.

When you are writing about your *current* position, use present tense in your verbs:

> • Support the planning / execution of USPACOM exercises throughout the Asia Pacific region. Facilitate small group, focused problem-solving discussions by senior civilian and military leaders of allied and partner nations.

But for your *previous* jobs, use past tense for your entries:

> • Supported the planning / execution of USPACOM exercises throughout the Asia Pacific region. Facilitated small group, focused problem-solving discussions by senior civilian and military leaders of allied and partner nations.

The suggestions in this chapter aren't deal breakers if you don't follow them…they just assist you in providing a more professional-looking resume…so I would suggest you use them!

**Resume Language checklist**

_____ Is the language in your resume too informal?

_____ Have you made sure typos do not exist in your resume?

_____ Have you eliminated pronouns (I, me, we, our, etc.) from your resume?

**Resume shorthand is okay to use**

\_\_\_\_\_ Are you using resume shorthand?

\_\_\_\_\_ Do you use present tense for your current job responsibilities and past tense for previous positions?

## Resume Formats

*Paper is a uniquely beautiful format, more so than the web, I think: you need to invest in the aesthetics.*

Dave Eggers

If you have been at this resume-writing game long at all (and even if you haven't been at it very long!), you may be aware that there are essentially three formats for resumes on the market these days. While there are variations on these themes, these are basically the primary formats of resumes you'll run into:

- Functional

- Chronological

- Combination

Let's talk about each of these kinds of resumes, and discuss when you may want to use them – or not!

### Functional Resume

The functional resume is basically a resume that lists all your skills, background and experience in groups at the beginning of your resume. Some functional resumes completely omit the companies where the experience of the candidate was gained.

Using my own resume, and abbreviating it a bit, following is an example of a portion of what a functional resume would look like:

# W. DANIEL QUILLEN

Street Address, City, State & Zip Code     303-555-1212     wdanelquillen@gmail.com

## SUMMARY

Senior Human Resource professional with a record of documented achievement and measurable performance in various industries. Strategic leader committed to providing best-in-class Human Resources support. Seasoned leader with impeccable ethics and integrity.

## SKILLS AND ACCOMPLISHMENTS

### HR Skills

• Legal compliance strengths protected the firm from law suits over employment law issues.

• Skillfully handled mergers and acquisitions, gracefully integrating individuals from multiple firms into the firm's culture.

• Strong employee relations skills, which prompted on retiring employee to say: "Dan put the human back in Human Resources."

• Investigated and resolved all employee complaints of hostile work place, gender discrimination, sexual harassment, EEOC claims, etc. Resolved all complaints satisfactorily for the complainant and the firm.

### Training and Mentoring Skills

• Guided the summer associate program, an internship opportunity for law school students at the firm. Program helped the firm evaluate and hire the best possible talent for the firm.

• Developed, launched and administered a voluntary staff and paralegal development program designed to enhance staff skills, improve client service and enrich the work experience for employees.

• Designed and implemented an organization-wide learning curriculum for managers. Resulting programs identified competency gaps and provided customized learning curricula for managers. Efforts hailed by company executives as break-through, creative and highly efficient.

***Recruiting Skills***

• Designed a recruiting strategy for a 16,000-employee business unit, aimed at recruiting and selecting only "A" players into our business. Business unit strategy was so successful it served as a model for corporate-wide recruiting.

• When the Director of Legal Recruiting left the firm, was asked to take over those responsibilities while maintaining Director of HR responsibilities until a suitable candidate could be found. Saved the firm over $250,000 in salary expense.

## EDUCATION

**Master of Business Administration, with Human Resource specialization**
Concordia University Wisconsin (Mequon, Wisconsin)

**Bachelor of Science in Business Administration, with Marketing minor**
Thomas Edison State College (Trenton, New Jersey)

As a hiring manager or recruiter, I might like the experiences and accomplishments listed, but I would be concerned about the information that's not there – the companies for whom this candidate worked, the dates at these companies, etc.

This is my least favorite format for resumes, and most hiring managers and recruiters don't like – nor trust -- these kinds of resumes either. Why? Because they tend to be used by job seekers who are trying to mask gaps or other concerns in their employment history.

I would be surprised to find a hiring manager who would be comfortable bringing in a candidate for an interview who didn't list the companies for whom they worked, or if listed, did so without the months and years of their time at each company.

Even if you have gaps in your employment, I would not use a functional resume. I have covered it here so that you are aware of it, but do not recommend its use.

## Chronological Resume

The chronological resume format is almost what it seems...perhaps a better term would be reverse-chronology format – your jobs are listed in reverse chronological order – you begin with your most recent job, with each previous job appearing after that.

Each job entry will include the name of the company for which you worked, your job title, the location of the company, dates of employment, responsibilities and accomplishments achieved while working for each employer.

I have used my resume again in an abbreviated manner to demonstrate this kind of resume format:

# W. DANIEL QUILLEN

Street Address, City, State & Zip Code      303-555-1212      wdanelquillen@gmail.com

## SUMMARY OF QUALIFICATIONS

Senior Human Resource professional with a record of documented achievement and measurable performance in various industries. Strategic leader committed to providing best-in-class Human Resources support. Seasoned leader with impeccable ethics and integrity.

## PROFESSIONAL EXPERIENCE

**Director of Internal Services**                                      **January 2013 to present**
City of Aurora, CO

- Promoted to Director of Internal Services. Responsible for management and direction of Human Resources, Risk Management, Purchasing and Fleet Operations for the City of Aurora.

- Part of a small team responsible for developing and implementing a broad succession planning program at the city. Results included the attraction and retention of stellar employees.

- Led the effort to replace the compensation and job classification structure for all city positions. Established market pay for employees across all positions at the City, ensuring the ability to recruit and retain employees.

**Division Manager of Human Resources**                  **November 2011 to January 2013**
City of Aurora, Colorado

- Effectively managed Employment & Compensation, Benefits, Recruiting and Training teams for the City of Aurora and its 3,700 employees, including 1,000 seasonal / temporary workers.

  o Introduced new recruiting strategies and tactics that effectively lowered the response time to our internal customers and candidates.

  o Led the performance management program for the city, directing the efforts of managers across the city, ensuring all employees received performance reviews and appropriate pay treatment.

**Director of Human Resources**                  **August 2001 to August 2011**
Holme Roberts & Owen LLP, Denver, CO

- Protected the firm from lawsuits by handling all disciplinary actions up to and including terminations using sound employment law practices. Over the course of ten years and 200+ terminations, there were no lawsuits filed against the firm for employment actions.

- Effectively managed all health benefits for the firm. Over a five-year period, negotiated more than $2,000,000 in savings for the firm while maintaining one of the best benefits packages in our market (excellent benefits, low deductibles, moderate premiums, etc.).

**Senior Human Resources Manager**                  **1998 to 2001**
Avaya / Lucent Technologies, Westminster, CO

- Due to success in complex HR situations, was asked to provide HR support to 1,400 Avaya Labs (formerly Bell Labs) scientists, a large department with significant complexity to their HR work (organizational development, recruiting, retention, compensation, etc.).

- Designed and implemented an organization-wide learning curriculum for managers. Resulting programs identified competency gaps and provided customized learning curricula for managers. Efforts hailed by company executives as breakthrough, creative and highly efficient.

## EDUCATION

**Master of Business Administration, with Human Resource specialization**
Concordia University Wisconsin (Mequon, Wisconsin)

**Bachelor of Science in Business Administration, with Marketing minor**
Thomas Edison State College (Trenton, New Jersey)

Chronological resumes are popular with managers and recruiters. They represent a familiar pattern; managers and recruiters can quickly scan the resume and see your experience, whether there are any gaps in your employment, etc.

## Combination Resume

The combination resume is exactly what it sounds like – it is a combination of elements of the functional resume (skills and accomplishments) and the chronological resume (listing of jobs, info about each employer and information about tasks and responsibilities of the position).

Again, using my abbreviated resume, I have demonstrated what a combination format looks like:

# W. DANIEL QUILLEN, SPHR

Street Address, City, State & Zip Code     303-555-1212     wdanelquillen@gmail.com

## SUMMARY OF QUALIFICATIONS

Senior Human Resource professional with a record of documented achievement and measurable performance in various industries. Strategic leader committed to providing best-in-class Human Resources support. Seasoned leader with impeccable ethics and integrity. Strengths include:

| | | |
|---|---|---|
| • Legal Compliance | • Succession Planning | • Organizational Development |
| • Talent Acquisition | • Employee Development | • Strategic HR |
| • Employee Relations | • Policy & Procedure Development | • Benefits |

## PROFESSIONAL EXPERIENCE

**<u>Director of Internal Services</u>**                           **January 2013 to present**
City of Aurora, CO

> • Promoted to Director of Internal Services. Responsible for management and direction of Human Resources, Risk Management, Purchasing and Fleet Operations for the City of Aurora.

- Part of a small team responsible for developing and implementing a broad succession planning program at the city. Results included the attraction and retention of stellar employees.

- Led the effort to replace the compensation and job classification structure for all city positions. Established market pay for employees across all positions at the City, ensuring the ability to recruit and retain employees.

**Division Manager of Human Resources**　　　　　**November 2011 to January 2013**

City of Aurora, Colorado

- Effectively managed Employment & Compensation, Benefits, Recruiting and Training teams for the City of Aurora and its 3,700 employees, including 1,000 seasonal / temporary workers.

  o Introduced new recruiting strategies and tactics that effectively lowered the response time to our internal customers and candidates.

  o Led the performance management program for the city, directing the efforts of managers across the city, ensuring all employees received performance reviews and appropriate pay treatment.

**Director of Human Resources**　　　　　**August 2001 to August 2011**

Holme Roberts & Owen LLP, Denver, CO

- Protected the firm from lawsuits by handling all disciplinary actions up to and including terminations using sound employment law practices. Over the course of ten years and 200+ terminations, there were no lawsuits filed against the firm for employment actions.

- Effectively managed all health benefits for the firm. Over a five-year period, negotiated more than $2,000,000 in savings for the firm while maintaining one of the best benefits packages in our market (excellent benefits, low deductibles, moderate premiums, etc.).

**Senior Human Resources Manager**　　　　　**1998 to 2001**

Avaya / Lucent Technologies, Westminster, CO

- Due to success in complex HR situations, was asked to provide HR support to 1,400 Avaya Labs (formerly Bell Labs) scientists, a large department with significant complexity to their HR work (organizational development, recruiting, retention, compensation, etc.).

- Designed and implemented an organization-wide learning curriculum for managers. Resulting programs identified competency gaps and provided customized learning curricula for managers. Efforts hailed by company executives as breakthrough, creative and highly efficient.

## EDUCATION

**Master of Business Administration, with Human Resource specialization**
Concordia University Wisconsin (Mequon, Wisconsin)

**Bachelor of Science in Business Administration, with Marketing minor**
Thomas Edison State College (Trenton, New Jersey)

Of the three formats, my favorite is the combination format resume – the resume that combines the strengths of the chronological resume and the skills focus of the functional resume – but without the weaknesses of the latter.

**Choose either the Chronological or Combination format**

Having said that, I think both the chronological and combination resumes are the strongest formats…if anything, **I favor the combination resume over the chronological**, since it allows you to highlight your primary skills and accomplishments in a separate section at the beginning of the resume, without forcing the hiring manager to search them out.

In later chapters we'll discuss each section of the combination resume, its value and how best to accentuate the positive aspects of your employment history, your skills and experience.

### Resume Language checklist

_____ Become familiar with the three primary resume formats: functional, chronological and combination functional and chronological.

_____ Decide which format best meets your needs.

_____ Write your resume in chronological and combination formats, and see which format you prefer.

_____ Regardless of the format you use, are you presenting yourself in the clearest, most succinct and professional manner possible?

# RESUME FORMATS

_____ Try creating combination and chronological resumes, and alternate submitting them for jobs. Track the responses you receive for interviews – is there a difference between formats? If so, use the preferred format more often.

_____ Can the hiring manager tell at a glance what you do, the kind of job you are seeking and can do?

## One Size Doesn't Fit All

*If you are out to describe the truth, leave elegance to the tailor.*
Albert Einstein

This is a chapter I hope you will take most seriously. It may make the difference between getting a job and languishing for months without one.

Now that I have your attention!

I was one of many Americans who lost their job during the Recession and discovered first-hand what it was like to seek work in the New Economy. I discovered very quickly that searching for work in the New Economy was very different than the last time I had actively searched for work – in the late 1970s. I found:

- many candidates for each job;

- over-worked hiring managers, recruiters and HR departments;

- applications software whose primary purpose was to screen out resumes (and applicants).

Currently I work for the City of Aurora, Colorado. Each Monday morning members of our HR department provide a benefits orientation for our newest city employees. Every Monday morning I take a few minutes and welcome each new group of employees to the city.

Prior to meeting with these new employees, I go to our applications software and pull up all the jobs that have been filled by this particular group of employees. Then, when I meet with them, I let each person know how many candidates they beat out to win their job. During the last calendar year, the average number of applicants we had for positions was 157, and that did not include our Fire and Police departments, which often receive over 2,000 applications for a handful of openings.

I share this information with you, not to discourage you, but to help you understand how important it is for you to stand out as a candidate. In years' past, if you had a squeaky clean resume with no typos or grammar difficulties, often that was enough to make you stand out from other applicants. That is no longer the case – most candidates today have squeaky clean resumes.

Your resume has to be top notch. It still has to be squeaky clean, but it also has to be specifically relevant to the position you are seeking. It has to be written in a way that will allow it to successfully make it through applications software.

Let me pause and speak briefly about applications software. Because HR departments are a mere shadow of the size they used to be years ago, and because there are often hundreds of applicants for each position, HR departments have resorted to applications software to help them screen resumes. Not knowing about applications software and what it does may cause your resume to be diverted, and the hiring manager will never see your resume, even though you may be the most qualified candidate for the position.

When you go to apply for a position and you are directed to input your resume online into a system, you are using applications software. Its purpose, to be quite brutally honest, is to screen your resume out of the horde of resumes that are received. It has been programmed by HR departments to search resumes on key words – Bachelors, Masters, MBA, training, sales, recruiting, talent acquisition, succession planning, strategic business, business-to-business, etc., are just a few of literally thousands of search terms that may be used to try and eliminate you from competition. If those words and others are not present in your application and resume, it will likely never be seen by human eyes.

Don't believe me? Let me give you a concrete example I used in *Get a Job!* I was up late (actually early) in the wee hours of the morning, searching for opportunities. I came across a job ad I had seen before, and had decided I wasn't interested. This time, however, I thought, "Why not?" and decided to apply. I printed off the job ad, highlighted the key words and experience they were seeking, and tailored my resume for the position. I wasn't a perfect fit for the job, but I had the vast majority of the skills and experience they were seeking. At 2:46am I submitted my application.

At 2:46am I received an e-mail in my Inbox from that company, acknowledging my submission. Among other things, it told me:

> **Your background, skills and experience will be reviewed against the position you have selected.**

At 2:56am – exactly ten minutes later – I received a rejection e-mail, which included the following:

> **Your background and qualifications have been given careful review with respect to this position. Although you were not selected for this position we appreciate your desire to expand your career.**

I know HR departments are over-worked and work long hours, but I am certain it wasn't an HR person who gave my resume a "careful review" between 2:46am and 2:56am on that Monday morning in July! As I mentioned, my experience was not a perfect fit for the job, and the applications software obviously thought so as well. In its review of my resume, it did not see a key word or key words it was looking for, and the result was my rejection as a candidate.

In this New Economy with hundreds of applicants for each job, one of the quickest and easiest ways for HR departments to screen resumes is on education. You will most likely be asked if you have a bachelor's degree (or master's degree, if that is what they are seeking). If you do not, you cannot lie, of course. But when you check that *No* box, you run the chance of not having your resume reviewed any further. What do you do then? Well – you try to find the name of the hiring manager and get him or her your resume directly. If s/he sees your skills and experience, they may waive the education requirement (a number of jobs require a bachelor's degree, or equivalent experience). But applications software may not allow you through the gate if it doesn't see a bachelor's degree listed on your resume.

Also, if you can have someone in your network reach out to the hiring manager, you may be able to overcome this obstacle.

Do NOT ignore the probability that your resume may be turned away by applications software. For that reason alone, you must tailor every resume to every job for which you apply. It is simply not possible for you to develop a resume that covers every possible key word for every job you are interested in.

**Assume my resume will be reviewed by applications software**

As you tailor your resume, also use the company's language. If you have recruiting experience, but the job ad says they are looking for *talent acquisition* experience, then that is the language you need to use in your resume. Now, you'd think that most HR departments will also program in the key word "recruiting" into the applications software, but why take the chance?

If your resume passes the applications software hurdle, within seconds it has to grab the attention of whoever is screening the resume – whether it is an HR department, recruiter, or hiring manager. And to do that, you must make the screener's job easy – you want to provide them with a resume that makes them say,

> **"My goodness – this person has already been doing what our job is! We need to get them in here right away for an interview!"**

How do you do that? Read on and learn.

When I lost my job, I began applying for jobs. I found that I was getting one interview for every four resumes I sent out. Networking groups I was part of were astounded – most members of those groups were getting one interview for every 20 or 25 resumes they sent out. Leaders of those networking groups asked me to come and talk about what I was doing to render such great success.

And that's just what I did. My formula was simple: I told them I tailored each resume to every job for which I applied. Following is the step-by-step process I followed.

**Craft a Basic Resume Template – Sections Only**

As I began to build my resume, I first identified the type of resume I wanted to use (see the *Resume Formats* chapter). Because I think it is the strongest format, I chose the combination functional / chronological format. Then I decided which sections I wanted to use in my resume. Here are the sections I chose:

- Heading / Resume Title

- Summary of Qualifications / Strengths

- Professional Experience

- Awards and Honors

- Education

- Certifications

After selecting those sections, I created a template, with only those sections and some initial formatting included:

# W. DANIEL QUILLEN, SPHR

Street Address, City, State & Zip Code      303-555-1212      wdanelquillen@gmail.com

---

## SUMMARY OF QUALIFICATIONS

---

## PROFESSIONAL EXPERIENCE

---

---

### AWARDS / HONORS

---

### EDUCATION

---

### CERTIFICATIONS

---

**Identify Skills, Experience, and Accomplishments for Each Section**

After establishing my template, I selected a number of entries that accurately represented my **skills, experience and accomplishments (SEAs)** for each section, and I inserted them into the various sections of the resume. This created a good, general / generic resume that I can use if I don't have a job ad to identify specific SEAs I should highlight. I could use this if a recruiter asked for my resume, even though s/he didn't have a specific job in mind for me. I would let that recruiter know that before s/he submitted my resume, I would like for him / her to let me know a little about the job for which they were submitting, so I could tailor the resume toward that particular job (they will understand!). Here's what my generic resume looks like:

# W. DANIEL QUILLEN, SPHR

Street Address, City, State & Zip Code     303-555-1212     wdanelquillen@gmail.com

---

### SUMMARY OF QUALIFICATIONS

---

Senior Human Resource professional with a record of documented achievement and measurable performance in various industries. Strategic leader committed to providing best-in-class Human Resources support. Seasoned leader with impeccable ethics and integrity. Strengths include:

| | | |
|---|---|---|
| • Legal Compliance | • Succession Planning | • Organizational Development |
| • Talent Acquisition | • Employee Development | • Strategic HR |
| • Employee Relations | • Policy & Procedure Development | • Benefits |

---

## PROFESSIONAL EXPERIENCE

---

**<u>Director of Internal Services</u>**                                 **January 2013 to present**

City of Aurora, CO

- Promoted to Director of Internal Services – responsible for management and direction of Human Resources, Risk Management, Purchasing and Fleet Operations for the City of Aurora. (This position is equivalent to Director or Vice President of Administration in the private sector.)

- Part of a small team responsible for developing and implementing a broad succession planning program at the city. Results included the attraction and retention of superior employees.

- Led the effort to replace the compensation and job classification structure for all city positions. Established market pay for employees across all positions at the City, ensuring the ability to recruit and retain employees and to pay them competitive market salaries.

**<u>Division Manager of Human Resources</u>**              **November 2011 to January 2013**

City of Aurora, Colorado

- Effectively managed Employment & Compensation, Benefits, Recruiting and Training teams for the City of Aurora and its 3,700 employees, including 1,000 seasonal / temporary workers.

  o Introduced new recruiting strategies and tactics that effectively lowered the response time to our internal customers and candidates.

  o Led the performance management program for the city, directing the efforts of managers across the city, ensuring all employees received performance reviews and appropriate pay treatment.

**<u>Director of Human Resources</u>**                                  **August 2001 to August 2011**

Holme Roberts & Owen LLP, Denver, CO

- Protected the firm from lawsuits by handling all disciplinary actions up to and including terminations using sound employment law practices. Over the course of ten years and 200+ terminations, there were no lawsuits filed against the firm for employment actions.

- Frequent changes within the firm required effective employee relations and interpersonal skills. Mergers, acquisitions, and recession-related changes in firm policy and guidelines all required extensive ability to inspire and retain employees. As demonstration of success in these areas, one retiring employee observed, *"Dan put the human back in Human Resources."*

• Effectively managed all health benefits for the firm. Over a 5-year period, negotiated over $2,000,000 in savings while maintaining one of the best benefits packages in the industry.

• Developed and revised many Human Resources processes and procedures, including performance management, employee development / training curricula and programs, paid leave / PTO, sabbatical, maternity and paternity leave, etc. This effort provided competitive and attractive policies and procedures allowing the firm to attract and retain top talent.

## Senior Human Resources Manager                    1998 to 2001

Avaya / Lucent Technologies, Westminster, CO

• Due to success in complex HR situations, was asked to provide HR support to 1,400 Avaya Labs (formerly Bell Labs) scientists, a large department with significant complexity to their HR work (organizational development, recruiting, retention, compensation, etc.). Earned *Exceeded* and *Far Exceeded* ratings and performance bonuses for work with this group.

• Designed and implemented an organization-wide learning curriculum for managers. Resulting programs identified competency gaps and provided customized learning curricula for managers. Efforts hailed by company executives as breakthrough, creative and highly efficient.

## Human Resources Generalist                    1992 to 1998

Lucent Technologies / AT&T, Greenwood Village, CO

• Certified as a Competency Consultant. Because of success in this area, was asked to work with a small team to introduce competency modeling company-wide (32,000 employees), including international locations.

• Led the international HR effort of the organization, including working effectively with the employment laws for Ireland, England, Germany, Singapore, Hong Kong, Tokyo and Australia. Was successful in this effort, protecting the company and making sure hiring, performance management and compensation practices met the requirements of the international communities.

---

## AWARDS / HONORS

---

• "Dan communicates very well; he knows when to talk and write like an employment lawyer, and when to talk and write like a Director of Human Resources." (Written comment in performance review by an employment law partner with whom I worked extensively.)

• Participant in "fast track" program for executives who exhibit extraordinary leadership potential. (Fewer than 2% of AT&T's employees are given this opportunity.)

• Freelance author. Sixteen books and several articles in national magazines published.

• Consistently rated *Exceeds* or *Far Exceeds* during performance management meetings.

## EDUCATION

**Master of Business Administration, with Human Resource specialization**
Concordia University Wisconsin (Mequon, Wisconsin)

**Bachelor of Science in Business Administration, with Marketing minor**
Thomas Edison State College (Trenton, New Jersey)

## CERTIFICATIONS

**Certified as Senior Professional in Human Resources (SPHR)**, Society for Human Resource Management.

**Certified as Competency Consultant** (McLagan Process)

Note that at the end of the **Summary of Qualifications** section, I list nine strengths. Those strengths should come *directly* from the job ad you are reviewing – those along with your *Summary* statement are the beginning of the process of tailoring your resume.

### Create a Resume Template for All Skills, Experience, and Accomplishments

I opened my general / generic resume and saved it as a resume template. In each section, I added all the SEAs I could think of that pertained to my background and experience. Each time I ran into a job ad that required me to craft another SEA entry, I entered that SEA in my template as well. My resume template eventually grew to include more than three dozen SEAs that I could pick and choose from to tailor my resume. I won't list all 37 in my resume template, but here are a few examples:

1.  Protected the firm from lawsuits by handling all disciplinary actions up to and including terminations using sound employment law practices. Over the course of ten years and 200+ terminations, there were no lawsuits filed against the firm for employment actions.

2.  Investigated and resolved all employee complaints of hostile work place, gender discrimination, sexual harassment, EEOC claims, etc. Resolved all complaints satisfactorily for the complainant and the firm. During ten-year tenure, not one lawsuit was filed against the firm.

3.  As part of an employee engagement and retention effort, developed, launched and administered a voluntary staff and paralegal development program designed to enhance staff skills, improve client service and enrich the work experience for employees. Ongoing classes supported and attended by over 90% of staff. Hailed as a significant success by firm management.

4.  Designed, developed, launched and administered a voluntary staff and paralegal development program designed to enhance staff skills, improve client service and enrich their work experience. Ongoing classes supported and attended by over 90% of staff. Hailed as a significant success by firm management.

5.  Implemented overtime guidelines that saved the firm over $750,000 over a two-year period while at the same time maintaining high levels of client service. This effort improved per-partner revenues, allowing us to attract and retain partners.

6.  Frequent changes within the firm required effective employee relations and interpersonal skills. Mergers, acquisitions, and recession-related changes in firm policy and guidelines all required extensive ability to inspire and retain employees. As demonstration of success in these areas, one retiring employee observed, "Dan put the human back in Human Resources."

7.  Led all staff and paralegal recruiting. Sourced, interviewed and hired candidates. Ensured candidates had required skills and cultural fit for the firm. Extremely low turn-over rate among new hires resulted in excellent client service and an efficient and productive work force.

8.   Effectively managed all health benefits for the firm. Over a five-year period, negotiated over $2,000,000 in savings for the firm while maintaining one of the best benefits packages in our market (excellent benefits, low deductibles, moderate premiums, etc.).

Note in particular entries #1 and #2 and #3 and #4. Both 1 & 2 and 3 & 4 are very similar entries, but each one was tailored – used the same or similar language – to what I found the hiring manager was seeking in the job ad. I would not use both of these entries in the same resume – they are just slightly different representations of a similar SEA. In other words, if I used entry #1, I would not use entry #2, and if I used entry #3, I would not use entry #4 (or vice versa). The point is, I want my resume to use as similar a language as I can to the job requirements I find in the job ad. (**Note** – I applied numbering to the above entries for ease of reference for this chapter. In your resume, do not use the numbers.)

**Review Job Ads, Then TAILOR Your Resume to Each Ad**

Speaking of the job ad – this is a most important step in tailoring your resume for each job. When I find a job I am interested in, I read it through for a general understanding of the job and its duties and requirements. As I read, I am going through a mental checklist to see if I have the SEAs they are looking for. If I feel there is a match, or if I meet most of the criteria they have listed, I print the job ad.

Once the job ad is printed, I read it more carefully now. Using a yellow highlighter, I highlight all the key words and phrases of the skills, experience and accomplishments they are seeking. Once completed, I should have somewhere between six and twelve SEAs that I can use to begin building the resume that matches the job description.

Following is the job ad for a position for which I applied. I have **highlighted** the SEAs (skills, experience, and accomplishments) I felt the hiring manager was looking for:

**Company**: Pearson Assessment

**Position**: HR Business Partner

**Job Description**: Pearson has one defining goal: to help people progress in their lives through learning. We champion innovation and we invest in models for education that deliver on our promise for effective, accessible, and personal learning from early literacy, college and career readiness to professional education, through data-informed instruction and inventive applications for mobile and digital learning.

Pearson, the world's leading learning company, has **global-reach** and market-leading businesses in education, business, and consumer publishing and is listed on the London and New York stock exchanges (UK: PSON; NYSE: PSO).

As a strategic partner, the HR Business Partner **aligns business objectives with employees and management** in designated business units. The HR Business Partner **serves as a consultant to management** on Human Resource related issues. The successful HRBP acts as **employee champion**, and assesses and anticipates HR-related needs. **Communicating needs proactively** with our HR department and business management, the HRBP **seeks to develop integrated solutions**. The HRBP formulates partnerships across the HR function to deliver value-added service to management and employees that reflect the business objectives of the organization. Maintain an effective level of **business literacy** about the business unit's financial position, its mid-range plans, its culture and its competition.

The HR Business Partner will maintain **in-depth knowledge of legal requirements** related to day-to-day management of employees, **reducing legal risks** and ensuring **regulatory compliance. Partner with legal department** as needed/required.

So from that job ad, I gleaned the following responsibilities / SEAs:

- Global reach

- Aligns business objectives with employees and management

- Serves as consultant to management

- Employee champion

- Partners with legal

- Communicates proactively

- Seeks to develop integrated solutions

- Reduces legal risks

- Strong business acumen

- In-depth knowledge of legal requirements & regulatory compliance

- Partners with legal department

Scanning that list, I feel very good – I have experience in each of those areas, and can legitimately consider each of those areas as some of my HR strengths. In my **Summary of Qualifications / Strengths** section, I then modify my Summary slightly to reflect these things, and I choose to include the following nine items to list as my strengths:

| | | |
|---|---|---|
| • Global HR | • Employee Advocate | • Legal Compliance |
| • Legal Partnership | • Oral & Written Communication | • HR Risk Reduction |
| • Management Consultant | • Strong Business Acumen | • Business Management Focus |

Armed with that information, I look over my list of resume entries in my resume template to see if I have any that reflect the SEAs they that the hiring company (Pearson Assessment) is looking for. Some include:

- Skilled in international Human Resources, including learning and working effectively within the employment laws for Ireland, England, Germany, Singapore, Hong Kong, Tokyo and Australia. Successful in this effort, protecting the firm and making sure hiring, performance management and compensation met the requirements of the international communities where we were located.

• Frequent changes within the firm required effective employee relations and interpersonal skills. Mergers, acquisitions, and recession-related changes in firm policy and guidelines all required extensive ability to inspire and retain employees. As demonstration of success in these areas, one retiring employee observed, "Dan put the *human* back in Human Resources."

• Coached department heads to ensure effective and efficient implementation of their business plans. This was done through timely and appropriate hiring, effective employee development and compensation structuring to attract and retain top talent whose skills matched the department's needs. This shortened the cycle time between ramp-up mode and full productivity.

As you can see, these entries cover Global HR, Employee champion / advocacy and consulting with management. I was fortunate to have experience – and therefore resume entries – for each of the nine areas of SEAs that Pearson was looking for.

And in my *Awards and Honors* section, I was able to add this entry:

> *"Dan communicates very well; he knows when to talk and write like an employment lawyer, and when to talk and write like a Director of Human Resources."* (Written comment in performance review by an employment law partner with whom I worked extensively.)

This entry directly addresses two of the SEAs Pearson was looking for: partnering with legal and being able to reduce HR risk.

Now, it's possible that you will come across jobs that you don't have entries or experience for each of the hot topics the company lists in their job ad. Don't let that bother you – if you can cover most of them, then do so. Sometimes, you'll find that the job ad is somewhat Spartan, and doesn't list a lot of specific SEAs they are looking for in the job. When that happens, address as many of those they do list in your resume, and then fill out the rest of your resume with your most impressive experiences, those that show you're not just some run-of-the-mill applicant.

**I must tailor my resume to each job!**

Let me make an important distinction here when it comes to tailoring your resume. **Do not cut sections of the job ad and paste them into your resume!** Hiring managers will see that and dismiss your resume as soon as they recognize what you have done (I would, anyway!). Use your own words to tailor your resume, not the company's job ad.

### Craft and Polish Your Resume

So, once you have identified and placed your entries in your resume, look it over carefully. Make sure you don't have two similar entries – it would not be good to do that. Check for typos, space between each paragraph and each section – spacing should be uniform throughout. When you are finished, step back for a few minutes and look at the resume critically – how does it "feel" – does it have plenty of white space (top, bottom, left and right margins), space between entries and sections? If not, perhaps you are trying to cram too much into your resume, and you need to take out an SEA or two. Remember – the jobs for which you place the most entries should be your most recent jobs. They should be longer entries than your jobs from 15 years' ago.

### Submit and Interview!

I began this chapter with the following short paragraph:

> **This is a chapter I hope you will take most seriously. It may make the difference between getting a job and languishing for months without one.**

I wasn't kidding when I said this. I also mentioned at the beginning of this chapter the success I had in getting interviews with my resumes (one out of four), versus many of my peers. Many of those individuals had similar credentials as me – years of experience in one industry or area of expertise, they had been laid off during the Recession, etc. And yet, even with excellent resumes, the best of them was getting one interview for every twenty resumes they sent out.

Does this system work? Yes it does. I have years of experience, and it worked for me. At the other end of the spectrum, it works for those without decades of experience. Not long ago, I became aware of a young-ish friend who was having a very difficult time finding a job. In fact, he had been out of work for nearly two years, and had basically given up his job search. He had great need for full-time (or any, for that matter!) employment, but he didn't have a lot of experience. I hadn't seen him for a number of years, but through a series of fortuitous events, he and I met again, and I became aware of his situation. I shared my job search experience in the New Economy, and we worked together to craft a basic resume for him. He learned how to tailor his resume, and followed my instructions – basically the instructions I have provided in this chapter. Within weeks of our working together, he was successful in finding work. The information I shared with him was from this book and *Get a Job!* Here is what he said about *Get a Job!* in his Amazon.com comments:

> *I was out of work for almost 2 years, and was just not getting many responses from the resumes I was sending out. I picked up a copy of Dan's book (Get a Job!) and began following his counsel in a number of areas, especially related to resumes and interviewing. Within 3 weeks, I had 4 interviews and received two job offers. I am now happily employed with a great job and feel like following Dan's counsel is the primary reason I was able to get these job offers and land my job.*

So please – take this chapter seriously. Craft your resume, tailor it to the job ad, send it off, and – if all goes well – interview for and win the job!

**One Size Doesn't Fit All checklist**

_____ Even though you are going to tailor your resume to each job, make sure your resume is squeaky clean. (No typos, grammar difficulties, formatting errors, etc.)

_____ Be sure to print and highlight the job ad for each job for which you wish to apply. Highlight the key skills, experience and accomplishments they are seeking.

_____ Develop a good generic / general resume for use when you do not know the details of a particular position. But that's the only time you want to use it! (Remember – one size does not fit all!)

_____ Develop a resume template that contains all the SEAs (skills, experience and accomplishments) you have. As you develop new SEA entries, add them to your template. You will use this to help you tailor resumes for jobs you are interested in.

_____ Learn how to get past applications software – tailor your resume, use key words from the job ad.

_____ Make the resume screener's job easy by tailoring your resume with only (or primarily) those skills and experiences they are seeking.

_____ After you have tailored your resume, make sure you have no typos, the spacing and formatting looks appropriate, etc.

_____ If you are concerned that your resume is being screened out because you haven't completed your bachelor's or master's degree, try to find who the hiring manager is and get them your resume directly, or enlist the aid of a member of your network to reach out to him or her.

**The Dead Moose on the Table**

*Euphemism is a human device to conceal the horrors of reality.*
Paul Johnson

Can we talk?

Sometimes there is a dead moose on the table, and you just have to acknowledge it, discuss it and move on.

What? You've never heard the term "the dead moose on the table?" Perhaps you have heard it phrased as the "the elephant in the room." Whichever beast you heard about (or not), neither the dead moose nor the elephant in the room can be ignored.

*A reference to elephants and dead moose is a euphemism.*

> Euphemism = exchanging a mild or vague phrase in the place of one that might be considered unkind, blunt or unnecessarily insensitive.

Either way, if you have a dead moose on your table as it relates to your resume or job hunt, you need to be aware of it, and address it. Ignoring the dead moose – which everyone sees and recognizes – does not make the dead moose go away; people are just polite and waltz around it, ever aware of its presence, but just not willing to address it head on.

What's the dead moose on your resume? Here are a few common ones:

- Little or no experience

- Gaps in employment

- Lack of Education

- A series of short employment opportunities

- Your age (old or young!)

Let's address of few of these more common issues that may be on your resume:

## Little or No Experience

Face it – the only way to get experience is, well, to get it – to experience it. Sometimes your lack of experience comes from your youth; and other times it has nothing do with your age – perhaps you are re-entering the work force after several decades of raising a family, or you are changing careers to an area in which you have limited experience. Whatever your situation, if you have little or no experience, you must do all you can to overcome the issue, and neutralize it as a consideration point for the hiring manager.

But how do you do that? Rather than speak of your weaknesses – your lack of experience – trumpet your strengths. Sometimes those strengths are directly related, sometimes you have to draw the connection for the interviewer. You've never sold widgets in the wack-a-doodle market before (that's your weakness)? Then replace it with a strength: while you are not familiar with widgets or their market, you were in a similar situation in your last job, and within 18 months, you became your company's top-producing salesperson. That is music to a hiring manager's ears!

But what if you not only have no experience selling widgets, but you have no experience at all with widgets, sales or the wack-a-doodle industry? What do you do then? You look for other skills, knowledge or attributes that will be of value to the organization with whom you are hoping to work.

I once interviewed a woman for a position for which she had only minimal qualifications – all of the other applicants had much more experience than she did. She fared well in the interview, notwithstanding her level of experience. But I was concerned about her lack of experience. Yet when I asked my final question, she knocked the ball out of the park. My question was, "We have a number of very qualified candidates; why should I hire you?" She straightened up in her chair, looked me in the eye, and said;

> *No one will work as hard as I will work, and no one will be as passionate as I am about this job! I love this work and will give it my very best every day!*

What's not to like about that answer?! (By the way – I hired her, and she proved to be one of the best hires I ever made!)

In her case, the strength she had to offer was not years and years of experience – in fact, that was the dead moose on *her* table – she offered up that which she had to offer – her passion and work ethic. After all was said and done, in her case – that was enough. Perhaps it will be for you.

Here's another example: When I was eighteen years old, I wanted to get a job in construction. I had no formal experience whatsoever (other than a few forts I had built in my back yard as an adolescent!). Time and again I was turned down for work because of my lack of construction experience.

Finally, I hit on a strategy. When I went for yet another interview, I decided to grab the dead moose by the antlers. Before we were very far into the interview, I said, "I know I do not have any construction experience. But I am a hard worker, and will give you all I can. I am a fast learner, and am certain I will be able to come up to speed quickly." And then to close the deal, I said, "I will even work for half wages until you feel I have learned enough to merit full pay." My interviewer – the owner of the small steel construction company with whom I was interviewing, seemed amused and intrigued. Said he: "How can I pass up an offer like that?!" And he hired me. (Note: notwithstanding my declaration of a willingness to work for half pay, to my owner's credit, he paid me full wages from Hour One.)

**Gaps in Employment**

In years' past, this was a particularly lethal dead moose on the table. However, in this New Economy, most hiring managers are more understanding of gaps than they used to be. They understand the last ten to fifteen years have been rough sledding economically, and that many excellent employees have been laid off through no fault of their own. But you must be prepared to confront this particular dead moose yourself and not rely solely on the good graces of the hiring manager.

There are several ways to do this. If you were part of a lay off that occasioned your departure and initiated the beginning of your employment gap – say so. Either on your resume or in your cover letter (both would be fine), share that information. I have seen resumes that said something like the following:

---

**Program Manager**                      **2008 – Oct. 2012**
XYZ Corporation

**Laid off as part of a 30% reduction in force due to recession and soft markets**.

- Responsible for all aspects of Project Management at XZZ Corporation

---

A tactic like this may help a hiring manager remember what a tough market it is, and you can demonstrate that you left the position through no reason that was within your control.

Another tactic is to fill any potential gap in employment with something – start your own consulting company, take temporary work through a temp agency, preferably in your area of expertise. So rather than a large gap between jobs, you can fill that time with some sort of employment. For example:

---

**Contract Project Manager**             **Nov. 2012 – Present**
Manpower, Inc.

Held a variety of contract project management positions for such companies as

What's the dead moose on my job-search table?

AT&T, Verizon, Johnson, etc. Responsibilities included:

> • Designed and implemented a project management schedule for a large expansion into new markets for AT&T.

---

Now doesn't that look better than having an employment gap between 2012 and now? As a special bonus, you'll be able to bring in a few extra shekels to help pay the bills while you are looking for other work.

When I was laid off from my law firm in 2011, friends recommended that I start an HR consulting company. Had I done so, I would have shown my company as I would any other job on my resume. If this is what you choose to do, I think it is important to actually form a company (most states charge only a reasonable fee to form a company – in Colorado it is $10) and seek to obtain clients. First of all – it's the honest thing to do. And second, it will strengthen your assertion that you actually did form a company if you can say that you provided HR consulting services for a number of companies.

Okay – so you are not a professional – HR, attorney, project manager, IT professional, etc. You are a car mechanic? Great – then form **Dave's Mobile Mechanic Service** and advertise on Craigslist, put flyers in supermarkets, hire young kids to deliver flyers door-to-door (or do it yourself with family members, etc., etc).

Do you have a friend or family member that owns a company that would give you a contract position, so that you can show that you were employed during that time? That's only an option if you actually do work for the company, but it is an option I know a number of friends and acquaintances have used. Even if it is only a few hours each week or month, you can use this on your resume.

Gaps in employment are not insurmountable, but you need to be prepared to put the best face on the situation as possible.

**Lack of Education**

If you have a lack of education in this market, you are climbing an uphill battle. My first counsel is: go get that education! There are scholarships and grants, student loans and many other sources for you to get your education. You have put it off this long, and now it is coming back to haunt you. While you are looking for work, now is a great time to go back and finish that degree you started twenty years ago. There are so many educational institutions out there that are geared toward adult education, look into them.

But – you need a job now, and I appreciate that. There are two tactics I can suggest for seeking work when you don't have the education that a lot of hiring companies are requiring: **Networking** and **Networking**.

Use your network to find out about jobs, and to then try to get members of your network to reach out to the hiring manager and say, "Hey – I know this person who would be a great employee for our company. She doesn't have her degree, but I think she'd be a rock star for us. Would you be willing to look at her resume?"

I have been hiring people for over two decades, and as good as I am, it is still scary to hire someone from a two-page resume and a 45-minute interview or two. If I can get a recommendation like that, you bet I will be willing to take a look at your resume.

So where do you find the people who can help you out? One of the best ways is through **social media** – especially **LinkedIn** and **Facebook**. Neither one requires an investment, and each can provide individuals who can assist you. When you join LinkedIn, begin connecting with as many people as you know – friends, neighbors, relatives, former work associates, school mates, etc. Once you've identified a job in which you are interested, go on LinkedIn and see if any of your connections works for that company. Just type in the company's name in the Search box on the main home page, and it will show you anyone in your network that works or worked at that company. If none of your first-level connections has work history at the company, it will show you anyone they are connected to who has an affiliation with that company. Perhaps they will be willing to put a good word in for you, on the recommendation of the mutual friend the two of you have.

While not as business focused, your friends on Facebook may be able to provide leads for you. In your status update, you can say something like: "Hey all, I am hoping to interview for a position with Acme Corporation here in Denver. Anyone out there have a contact at Acme I can speak with?" Once a conversation is started, perhaps your friend will introduce you to their friend, along with a positive recommendation.

Lack of education just makes the degree of difficulty of your job hunt a little higher, so you have to be a little more aggressive about certain aspects of your job hunt.

### Your Age (Old or Young)

It seems that if you are young in your career, or old in your career, there is a temptation to feel like all the older / younger workers are getting the opportunities, and that because of your youth / older age you are being passed over. There are things you can do to combat these prejudices.

For younger workers, can I just assure you that if I am willing to hire someone who is just out of college, or very new in their career, I understand you won't have a lot of experience. And that's okay. But – understand that as a new college grad with no more experience than a summer internship or two, you're not going to land a vice president position at a major company! It's not because of your age – it's because of your experience, or lack thereof. You will need to be content with starting your career where most of us older folks have – at or near the bottom of the ladder. The higher-paying jobs typically require at least some experience.

If you really are after the bigger bucks, you might consider sales positions in any of a number of industries. They will often bring on new college hires who don't have much experience, and train them the way they want them to be trained.

As you interview as a younger worker, accentuate the positive – your vigor, your excitement to finally be in the work force and your passion for the area of work you have chosen (communications, marketing, construction, etc., etc.). Stress your flexibility and willingness to learn.

Don't apologize for your youthfulness and lack of experience – capitalize on it. Once I was interviewing a group of individuals for an HR assistant position I had open. Two of them were from Spanish-speaking countries. Although their accents were noticeable, they spoke English very well. One of the candidates apologized numerous times during her interview about her accent. The other candidate, however, chose to be positive about it. She said something like: "You've probably noticed that I have an accent. I am a native of Mexico, and Spanish is my first language. This will be a benefit to you because I can communicate well with any Spanish-speaking employees or clients that you have." What a difference in those two approaches!

For older workers, yes, age discrimination is alive and well. That is why it is important for you to be cautious in what you reveal on your resume. If you include the job you got right out of college, it doesn't take much of a math expert to figure out that if you worked there beginning in 1969 that you are probably a few years beyond age 40 (50…60). That's why I recommend not including jobs past ten to fifteen years ago. Don't include your college graduation dates on your resume. Once you have gotten your interview, then is the time for you to wow them with your ability, experience and capabilities.

In *Get a Job!*, I explained a situation I had to deal with. A friend pointed out that while I was getting a lot of interviews, I was not landing any of the jobs. He suggested at least part of the reason was that I was being discriminated against because of my age. He suggested a unique approach I thought was brilliant. He suggested I prepare a short conversation about my age, and in it I would seek to dispel any concerns my potential hiring manager might have about older workers. With his guidance and advice, here is what I came up with. He suggested that near the end of my interview, when asked if I had any questions, or wanted to share anything with them, that I roll out my prepared comments.  Here's what I said:

> As you may have noticed, I am not a spring chicken, and I am probably older than most of the other applicants. But I want you to know that I have a lot of runway left on my career – I am not considering retirement any time soon. I have three children who are in college for a number more years, and besides, I am nowhere near being ready to retire.
>
> **(That dispels their concern that I will retire as soon as I get trained.)**

I am very good at learning new software. I have been at this so long that I have used many different software packages, and have never had difficulties picking up new applications or software packages.

**(That addresses any concerns they have about whether or not I can learn new software or work with new technology.)**

I enjoy all ages of workers and work well with younger workers as well as workers my age.

**(So much for the concerns about me being a grumpy old man…)**

And I am very healthy. I have worked 50 hours a week for most of my career, and have no reason to expect I will work less in this position.

**(And now they know I am healthy and they don't have to worry about me being sick all the time.)**

In addition, the benefit to you is that you get an HR professional with years of HR experience. I have been doing HR so long, there are very few things that surprise me – I have seen it all. Because of that, I don't get too excited or agitated about anything that comes up.

**(Adding a cherry on top – not only do they not have to worry about me as an older worker, but they actually benefit from it!)**

For the purposes of this book, I wish I could tell you I used this approach many times. But I didn't – I used it only once. But…I am batting 1000 when using it – I got every job for which I applied when I used that dialogue.

## Job Hopping

One thing hiring managers and HR professionals are wary about is a resume that has a lot of jobs in a short period of time, indicating the person may be a job hopper. You must guard against this in your career. I consider someone a potential job hopper if they have a

> **Meet age discrimination head-on**

history of staying at places less than two years. One or two of these short stops don't concern me, but if there are more than that, I do get concerned.

To get past that, if there are legitimate reasons for your departures, mention it both in your resume as well as your cover letter. I once interviewed a woman who appeared to be a job hopper. But her resume included the following comments on each of the jobs she'd had the previous few years:

- Company went through serious lay-offs, and since I was one of the last ones hired, I was one of the first to go.

- Company went out of business.

- Company moved the HR department to Illinois, and I was unwilling to move there.

- The partner for whom I was hired to work went to another firm, and he was unable to take me with him.

I checked out her story…and she was not fibbing – those things really happened at the companies she had worked for. Her job history prior to those four companies had been very strong, so I was willing to give her the benefit of the doubt

I interviewed one candidate who was totally unlike any other I interviewed. He had very good experience, but appeared to be a bit of a job hopper. When I asked him about it, he took me through his resume and said things like, "Well, I left this job to find myself. I toured South America for six months, and came back to the US with a new lease on life." Several other departures seemed to have good explanations, but when he told me he left another job to "find himself," I decided he wasn't the candidate for our company!

So – those are some of the more common dead mooses on tables that I have run into. Regardless of what your dead moose on the table is, you must develop a strategy on how to face it, defuse it, and even turn it into a strength, if possible. Hoping that no one will notice it, however, is not a good strategy!

**The Dead Moose on the Table checklist**

_____ Is there a dead moose on your job-searching table?

# THE DEAD MOOSE ON THE TABLE

_____ If you have a dead moose on your table, you need to devise a strategy to deal with it.

_____ Don't be dismayed – many candidates are successful even though they have a dead moose on their table.

_____ Accentuate the positive – look for ways to turn your dead moose into a positive, a strength, an asset for the company.

_____ Don't job hop!

_____ Don't be dismayed if you do have a dead moose on your job-search table. Just find a positive way to deal with it.

# 12   Section-by-Section Resume Review

*Twice and thrice over, as they say, good is it to repeat and review what is good.*

Plato

As you prepare your resume, you must pay special attention to all its elements. The key elements in a resume are:

- Heading / Resume Title

- Summary of Qualifications / Strengths

- Professional Experience

- Awards and Honors

- Education

- Certifications

Some resumes, like IT resumes, for example, may include additional sections, especially one exhibiting software skills, systems worked with, etc. Legal resumes may have separate sections that illustrate significant cases or transactions (real estate, IPOs, mergers & acquisitions, etc.). Academic resumes may include sections on grants received, course taught, research projects completed, etc.

Let me mention a few sections that are not in the list above.

# SECTION-BY-SECTION RESUME REVIEW

**Objective sections**. I am not a big fan of Objective sections, and if I receive a resume with such a section, I typically ignore the section completely. Unless someone has forgotten to change their objective and it says something like:

> Seeking to use my experience and skills in a management position in the healthcare industry.

That's all fine and good, except the position I have open is not in the healthcare industry! If I run across a resume with an *Objective* section like that, there are already 2.5 strikes against that candidate. I don't reject it outright, but close.

**Personal sections**. Again, I am not a fan of these sections. I may sound like a curmudgeon, so no offense, but I have absolutely zero interest in your hobbies, marital status, volunteer work or other such personal tidbits. You were a Division 1A collegiate or professional athlete? I'll admit that's impressive to me, broken-down old athlete that I am. But I would prefer to see information like that in an *Awards / Honors* section, or in your cover letter.

As I was writing *Get a Job!*, I reviewed a professional resume at work with the following *Personal* section:

> Married to Cindy, a ceramic artist and potter. We have two sons, Scott, a biologist and Anthony, a music teacher. My family and I enjoy swimming, biking, hiking, skiing, camping, climbing mountains, golf and most any outdoor activities. We also enjoy cultural experiences including art, music, and travel.

Now I am certain Cindy is a lovely woman, and Scott and Anthony are perfectly delightful children, but none of that is something I have the slightest bit of interest in as a hiring manager. (Note: names in the above paragraph have been changed…!)

The only exception I have run across in my review of tens of thousands of resumes is one fellow's *Personal* section that included the fact that he had led a blind climber up Kilimanjaro and Mt. Everest. Now *that* is something I found impressive!

**References Available Upon Request**. I wish I had a dollar for every resume I have reviewed with that unnecessary ditty appended at the end of a resume. That is assumed. I have yet to ask a candidate for their references and had them say, "No, I think not."

Okay, now that I have that out of my system, let's get to the resume sections I do believe are viable and important to have in your resume. I'll use sections of my resume to illustrate each of those sections.

**Heading / Resume Title section**

# W. DANIEL QUILLEN, SPHR

### Dan's LinkedIn profile

---

Nothing too exceptional here. I have centered my name, but I have also seen resumes with the name left- and right-justified that I thought looked fine. Try placing your name in different places to see which you like best.

You'll note **I have included a URL link to my LinkedIn profile** instead of including my address on this version of my resume. In today's social-media-conscious business world, I think this is a good move. For years the expectation was that you would include your address on your resume. However, there is a school of thought out there now that feels your home address may not be necessary, and in fact, may be used against you. I experienced this mindset in person a few years' ago. I was helping a partner of my law firm review resumes, and we came to one candidate I thought was pretty strong. But she dismissed her without even reviewing her resume. She said, "She lives an hour from our office – she'll never want to make that drive." So – it's your decision whether you want to include your address on your resume or not.

So you may want to use this opportunity to include a link to your LinkedIn profile. If the recruiter or hiring manager is reviewing your resume electronically, all they need do to reach your LinkedIn profile is click on your link, and voila! they are viewing your very professional LinkedIn profile. (Make sure it is professional and up to date!) And, if you create a hyperlink (instead of using the URL) to your LinkedIn profile, I think it looks a little cleaner!

I am not a fan of cell phones – I think their quality is abysmal in many cases. The last thing I want is to have a hiring manager call me and then be unable to communicate effectively because my cell phone keeps clipping – or dropping them. I prefer a home line. Of course, that means I don't receive calls when I am out of the house. Most people will call either leave a message or call back if they are interested.

Regardless of whether you use your cell phone or your home phone, make sure your voice mail greeting is pleasant and professional.

Can I just say a word or two about e-mail addresses? Please be judicious in the e-mail address you use. A few years ago my 110-year-old staid and stodgy law firm was advertising for an assistant controller. I received a number of resumes, and narrowed it down to a half dozen. I prepared to send e-mails to the applicants inviting them to come in for an interview, when I ran across this e-mail address of one of the finalists:

> One_Hot_Woman@_____.com

Amused, I shared the information with my boss. He laughed and said, "Well, we're not hiring her, but I want to interview her!" We both laughed about it. But we didn't call her in for an interview. (I called her to say she should probably change her e-mail address, that it likely didn't portray the image she was looking for.)

Seriously – e-mail addresses are cheap – they are free. Go to Gmail, Yahoo.com, Juno.com, etc., and find yourself a nice, safe e-mail.

I prefer to use e-mail to contact candidates, but I know many managers who prefer to call. I like using e-mail because in our 24/7 society, I can leave an e-mail and someone can respond at any time of the day or night. Other managers prefer to speak on the phone, to get a feel for the candidate that way.

If you do include your e-mail address, be sure and check it frequently. I once e-mailed a candidate who I thought had exceptional experience and background. I didn't hear from him. I e-mailed him again...and didn't hear from him. We proceeded with our interviews, and offered the job to one of the candidates. The next day I heard from the fellow I had e-mailed a week earlier, telling me he would be delighted to interview for the position. A...little...too...late. Enough said.

**Summary of Qualifications / Strengths section**

---

## SUMMARY OF QUALIFICATIONS

---

Senior Human Resource professional with a record of documented achievement and measurable performance in various industries. Strategic leader committed to providing best-in-class Human Resources support. Seasoned leader with impeccable ethics and integrity. Strengths include:

| | | |
|---|---|---|
| • Legal Compliance | • Organizational Design | • Multi-site HR |
| • Employee Relations | • Recruiting | • Interpersonal skills |
| • Benefits Expertise | • Employee Development | • Evaluations |

I mentioned earlier that I do not like *Objective* sections, but I do like a *Summary of Qualifications / Strengths* section. You'll note I have provided three sentences that summarize what kind of candidate I am:

> • seasoned HR professional;

> • lots of experience;

> • documented achievements with measureable performance;

> • have worked in various industries;

> • impeccable ethics and integrity.

Note the nine strengths I have listed. As you learned in the *One Size Doesn't Fit All* chapter, these should come *directly* from the job ad for the position in which you are interested.

**Professional Experience**

---

## PROFESSIONAL EXPERIENCE

---

<u>**Director of Human Resources**</u>                    **2001 to 2011**
Holme Roberts & Owen LLP, Denver, CO

  • Protected the firm from lawsuits by handling all disciplinary actions up to and including terminations using sound employment law practices. Over the course of ten years and 200+ terminations, there were no lawsuits filed against the firm for employment actions.

  • Used competency modeling expertise to assess required skills for positions, and identified skill gaps within the work force. Training curricula developed to address deficiencies within the various work groups, resulting in a more efficient and skilled work force.

  • Developed, launched and administered a voluntary staff development program designed to enhance staff skills and enrich their work experience. Ongoing classes supported and attended by over 90% of staff. Hailed as a significant success by firm management.

  • Effectively managed all health benefits for the firm. During a five-year period, negotiated over $2,000,000 in savings for the firm while maintaining one of the best benefits packages in the market (excellent benefits, low deductibles, moderate premiums, etc.).

  • Implemented overtime guidelines that saved the firm over $750,000 over a two-year period while at the same time maintaining high levels of client service. This effort improved per-partner revenues, allowing us to attract and retain partners.

  • Skilled at cultural transformation and organizational design. Over the past several years several firm mergers / acquisitions required effective cultural assimilation and organizational design. Efforts resulted in rapid employee and partner assimilation and a more efficient work force.

The *Professional Experience* section continues the tailoring of your resume. You want to match the experiences you include in your resume with those that are represented in the job ad. This is very important.

You should begin with your most recent position and work backwards. Unless you have worked for one of the 800-pound gorillas of Corporate America – IBM,

Microsoft, Apple, Google, etc. – your future employer will most likely be interested in **your job title**, not **the company** for which you worked. So that should be on the first line, and your company should be on the second line:

**Director of Human Resources**                                              **2001 to 2011**
Holme Roberts & Owen LLP, Denver, CO

instead of:

**Holme Roberts & Owen LLP, Denver, CO**                            **2001 to 2011**
Director of Human Resources

The listing for your length of service with a company should be done in years. Anything under two-ish years should be listed with months, like this:

**December 2007 – August 2009**

A listing of 2007 – 2009 could be as little as 13 months (December 2007 to January 2009) or as long as 24 months January 2007 to December 2009). For shorter jobs, if you don't list the month and year on your resume, expect to be asked for that information on an application or during an interview.

Remember – you used the job ad to determine what your nine bullet points in the *Strengths* section would be. Continue that effort by inserting the entries that address those same attributes in the *Professional Experience* section. Don't be satisfied with just tailoring the nine strengths to the job ad.

Be sure you include accomplishments in the entries in your *Professional Experience* section. You want your potential hiring manager to see that not only did you do the things s/he needs in the position they are trying to fill, but you did them well.

Tailoring your resume may seem like a lot of work. It is. But let me put it this way: You can apply for a job in five to ten minutes using a generic resume, and never hear back from the company, except perhaps a canned response that says, "Thanks, but no thanks." Or – you can spend an hour to ninety minutes sprucing up your resume and tailoring it to the specific job at hand, and increase your possibility of being interviewed four- or five-fold. The choice is yours…but what else are you doing with your time? What else is demanding your attention during these involuntary days off that are now part of your life? I happen to think tailoring each resume is a pretty good use of your time during this phase of your life.

And – here's some good news – as you create your resume template, filling it with tailor-made entries for each job, you will begin to get very good – and quick – at putting your resume together. It does get easier!

**Awards / Honors**

---

### AWARDS / HONORS

---

- *"Dan communicates very well; he knows when to talk and write like an employment lawyer, and when to talk and write like a Director of Human Resources."* (Written comment in performance review by an employment law partner with whom I worked extensively.)

- Participant in "fast track" program for executives who exhibit extraordinary leadership potential. (Fewer than 2% of AT&T's employees are given this opportunity.)

- Freelance author. Sixteen books and several articles in national magazines published.

- Published article on *Society for Human Resource Management* website: <u>Paralegals & the FLSA</u>.

- Wrote article for *The Colorado Lawyer*: <u>Making Healthcare Insurance Affordable for Your Firm</u>.

This is a section I strongly recommend. This section helps differentiate you from the crowd – help the hiring manager to see that you stand out among your peers. So you were a salesman – there are millions of them in America. Oh – you were *Salesman of the Year* for three years in a row? Earned fifteen *Salesman of the Month* awards during your two years with ABC Company? Tell that story! You can include it in the *Professional Experience* section as one of the bullet points, if you prefer, but I prefer it pulled out and highlighted in a special section like this. If you have only one such element, then it probably doesn't warrant a separate section; but if you have several, then put them here.

Use this section to highlight those activities you did that might be considered above and beyond the call of duty. Perhaps you were selected as your company representative at an important industry conference, or wrote a training manual that was adopted by your industry, or you wrote an article for an industry newsletter or website. You exceeded your sales quota every quarter for the past eight years. All these are activities and accomplishments you are proud of and set you apart from the unwashed masses – tell your story!

Note the first bullet point from this section. Even though it wasn't exactly an honor, I thought this was something I wanted a hiring manager to know about me, because I thought it spoke volumes about my abilities as a human resource professional. So look beyond the plaques and certificates and include things here that tell the hiring manager you are an accomplished and capable employee.

## Education

---

## EDUCATION

---

**Master of Business Administration, with Human Resource specialization**
Concordia University Wisconsin (Mequon, Wisconsin)

**Bachelor of Science in Business Administration, with Marketing minor**
Thomas Edison State College (Trenton, New Jersey)

As with the *Professional Experience* section, unless you graduated from one of the Top-Tier schools in the nation – Harvard, Princeton, Stanford, or Yale, for example – **lead with and bold your degree**. Do not include your dates of graduation – that allows a screener to determine your approximate age. Some applications software asks for it, but usually allows you to continue in the application without inputting it. I think it's just a wise practice to exclude that whenever possible.

If you graduated with honors – Summa Cum Laude, Cum Laude, etc., – include that. Similarly, if you had a high GPA – 3.9 or 4.0 – include that too.

If you attended a branch of a school, be sure and identify the branch / campus that you attended. Sometimes there is no difference in the schools, sometimes there is. If there is – perhaps the main campus has a more prestigious reputation than your campus – don't try to pass yourself off as a graduate of the main campus. A quick reference check or transcript requirement will indicate your dishonesty!

If you graduated from one of the Top-Tier schools in the nation, you may want to lead with that school in the *Education* section.

What do you do if you left school without completing your degree, or are still in school (whether full-time or evenings)? I would show that information, and if you have one, put an estimated graduation date. Here is an example:

**Candidate for Bachelor of Science in Business Administration, with Mathematics minor**

University of Colorado (Boulder, CO) (estimated graduation date: 6/1/20XX)

If you started college and didn't finish, I would include that:

**Candidate for Bachelor of Science in Business Administration, with Mathematics minor**

University of Colorado (Boulder, CO) (completed five semesters)

While that last is not as strong as having completed your degree, it is still better than no college at all. And – go back and finish! Even if you have to do it one class at a time, do it!

If you have no college or perhaps only one semester, I would not include an *Education* section in your resume.

If you have taken classes through your work or other venues, it is okay to add classes you think might be applicable to the position for which you are applying. But limit it to those that are directly relevant. However – don't take up valuable space in your resume just to include these classes. If you get to the end of your resume and have space remaining, I think it is fine to include these classes in the *Education* section.

Certifications / Memberships

---

## CERTIFICATIONS / MEMBERSHIPS

---

**Certified as Senior Professional in Human Resources (SPHR)**

**Certified as Competency Consultant** (McLagan Process)

Long-time member of the Board of Directors for the Mile High Association of Legal Administrators.

Include certifications that are specific to your industry or profession.

These are the basic sections you should have in your resume. Again, if you are in specialized profession than you may add other sections. Attorneys should have a section that covers Bar admissions or special transactions; IT professionals will often include the certifications they have or major systems they have expertise with, etc.

**Section-by-Section Resume Review checklist**

_____ No personal information in your resume (hobbies, number of children, names of family members, etc.).

_____ Use a professional e-mail address.

_____ No *Objective* section!

_____ Do not include dates of graduation from college.

_____ Show the month and year of your time at any jobs that were for shorter durations than two or three years.

_____ If you have some college, include it on your resume. Do not show which high school you graduated from.

_____ Include relevant certifications and association memberships.

# Resume Samples

*I'd update my resume so you're ready for any outcome.*
Bob Weinstein

Throughout the various chapters in this book, I have provided my thoughts, counsel and direction regarding resumes. We've talked about resume language, formats, mechanics, key words, appearance, accomplishments, sections and etc. In this chapter I will provide several sample resumes. I have varied the formatting on them so you can see there is no one "right" way. Feel free to choose any of these templates for your own resume, or even venture out on your own and draft your resume differently from these.

To give you a little variety to consider, I have provided examples of the following kinds of resumes:

- Military returning to private industry

- Las Vegas Gaming professional

- IT professional

- HR professional

- Top Executive resume

- Educator

I have some thoughts on each of these resumes, so I will spend a few paragraphs speaking about each one before we get to them.

**Military Returning to Private Industry Resume**

For all the men and women in the service (thank you for that service, by the way!), I have a few words of caution: You have learned and have been speaking a different language than most civilians! If your resume and cover letter have an avalanche of acronyms (USPACOM, CDRUSPACOM, MARFORPAC, CINCPAC, AOR, TS, SCI, UAV, SSO, JPAS, etc.), or a jungle of jargon (contingencies, tactical intel, theaters of operations, indigenous civilians, multi-INT), the recruiter's eyes will most likely glaze over as they quickly reach to place your resume in the "Thanks, but no thanks," pile. At a minimum, be sure and translate acronyms for your resume screener the first time you use them in your resume. And be careful of the jargon you use in your resume and your cover letter.

My friend Bryan is a Navy SEAL. He is transitioning to the private sector, and was not seeing any action with his resume, so he asked me to take a look at it. The first entry he had under his SEAL service was:

> Conducted unconventional warfare, counter-guerilla warfare, and clandestine operations in maritime and urban environments.

I explained to Bryan that most civilian hiring managers do not have a need for unconventional and counter-guerilla warfare or clandestine operations, either in a maritime *or* urban environment! Nor do they have the need for someone who can kill stealthily. So we brainstormed ways we might translate these experiences into something that would light up a civilian employer's eyes. We determined that his experience allowed him to creatively solve problems and overcome adversity and obstacles to achieve his objectives. While I think we can agree that's not as sexy as his original entry, it translates better into the civilian working world!

# RESUME SAMPLES

The first resume you'll come to after this section is for a military veteran seeking to transition to private industry.

## Las Vegas Gaming Professional Resume

I worked with a young gaming professional to put together his resume, and we looked for a way to soften his accomplishments from "take all our customers' money but make them feel good about it" to something a little less ominous. Seriously, not being a gambler, I am blissfully unaware of the language and culture associated with the Las Vegas community, so it was interesting to work with this young man to put together his resume.

You'll note that he doesn't have much experience beyond his gaming and serving experience, but we tried to display that service in the most interesting way possible.

## IT Professional Resume

IT resumes, like educators' resumes, often have sections that other resumes do not have. You may have noticed that among the many resume sections I mentioned, I did not talk about listing your technical / software skills (like Excel, Word, PowerPoint, etc.). However, most effective IT resumes will have a section for that information. It won't contain the basic Microsoft suite of products, however; it will most likely contain a host of programming languages, networking software, etc.

Most IT resumes will also have an extensive section containing certifications. IT professionals are this generations' shade-tree mechanics – no formal education necessary if you have the skills and aptitude for that business (I still advocate getting at least a Bachelor's degree, however, even in an IT field).

## Resume for a Youth with Little or No Experience

You will now find this resume in the Appendix. In the previous edition of this book, I included a resume for someone who has little or no experience in the workplace. Since then, I have a new book out especially for those of you (or for the children of people you know) who are about to join the workforce: *Your First Job: The Recent Grad's Indispensable Guide to Getting a Job.*

Are you still a student – haven't yet graduated from college? All the better! There are things you can do now that will help pave the way for when you do graduate, and if you are diligent you may be able to slip right from the graduation podium to the workplace.

You haven't yet gone to college? You're just graduating from high school and wonder what you should do? Can't decide whether you should work for a while before going to college? Or – should you go to college at all? Good – I have a chapter in that book specifically designed for you. So if you're about to embark on a career for the first time, pick up *Your First Job* and let me know what you think!

## HR Professional Resume

You've seen portions of my resume already in this book, but I thought I would share the entire thing in this chapter of resume samples. It demonstrates most everything we spoke about in the earlier chapters of this book – all the sections, accomplishments, etc.

I have a particular format I like for my resume, and you'll see it in this example. But I hasten to say it's not the only format you can use. Experiment a bit until you find the format and formatting that you feel best represents you. You'll note the format I prefer is the combined functional and chronological resume.

## Top Executive Resume

If you are a top executive seeking a position, the elements we have been talking about throughout this book apply to you and your resume. It must be perfect, it must show your skills and experience and that you were more than a caretaker executive – what accomplishments are yours? How did you move the company forward? Did you take them public, and made astounding profits for your investors? Then tell us!

Among all the resumes we have spoken about in this book, yours must be the epitome of excellence. It must exude professionalism and confidence. It must attract the eye of boards of directors, executive recruiters, etc. It must be the best it possibly can be.

## Educator Curriculum Vitae (CV)

Resumes for educators follow a pretty standard format, and they are a different format from most of the ones we have been talking about in this book. If you are reading this section, there is a good chance you are an educator. If that's the case, then you know that in the world of academia, resumes are generally referred to as curriculum vitae (Latin for *the course of my life*), or CV.

I have a friend who is the chair of his department at a major university. I asked for his thoughts on resumes (CVs) for individuals seeking positions at universities, and no surprise – his thoughts were basically the same as mine on the topic. He confirmed that notwithstanding the differences in basic resume format, many of the things discussed throughout this book are important / critical in education CVs. No typos or grammar errors. Attention to detail. Resume / CV shorthand, accomplishments and so on.

Like me, my friend abhors *Objective* sections. He insists that the cover letter is as important as the CV, and in some cases more important. For him, if you don't sell him on your candidacy in the cover letter, he doesn't waste time with your CV. I know many hiring managers in private industry who feel the same way.

He stressed the importance of knowing the university / college at which you are applying. You should learn what is important to them, and your CV should reflect that (sounds a lot like tailoring, doesn't it?!). If the university is a research university, your cover letter and CV had better contain information about your research skills, experience and successes. If they are a teaching university, then that is what your CV should reflect. If they are both, then that is what your CV should demonstrate.

He went on to say that he evaluates CVs looking for whether or not the candidate will "fit" their university. Your CV must reflect the key attributes that indicate that fit will be natural. He evaluates whether he thinks the candidate can do what they need them to do (research, teach classes, make major presentations, etc.), and whether they seem to have a genuine interest in becoming and remaining a part of their university community (in other words – they're not just looking to get their ticket punched and move on). He declared: "...if the CV doesn't pop regarding how they'll fit, then ho hum." (There's that need for attention to appearance and tailoring again.)

Generic CVs – those that try to be so broad they'll be accepted any place – find their way to the "Thanks, but no thanks" pile quickly.

He shared his aversion to *Personal* sections, practically quoting me verbatim (hmmm – speaking with him has me using Latin words…); here's what I said earlier:

> I may sound like a curmudgeon, so no offense, but I have absolutely zero interest in your hobbies, marital status, volunteer work or other such personal tidbits.

And that's essentially what he said as well. He did say he was interested in whether you had the skills to do the job he has open, and whether you had experience that was relevant to that position. He added that he is interested in skills that indicate that the candidate would add value to the department.

My friend shared additional information with me that I thought encapsulated so much of what I have been trying to say throughout this book, that I have included it below:

> For a school like ours that values both research and teaching, it's important that the CV reflect the fact that the candidate can do both well. A heavy researcher who isn't really interested in teaching, or an all-star teacher who just can't get around to doing scholarly work will not succeed at our institution, and if we sniff any evidence that such might be the case, we generally rank that candidate low. Our contracts also contain a significant 'service' component, so we need to see that the candidate will be a good citizen. We can't afford to hire someone who expects to sit in the Ivory Tower all day--- contributions to the college and department are crucial. In short, know what's expected of the job you're applying for, and be sure that you can deliver (and demonstrate it!).

As you turn to the last resume sample in this chapter – the Educator CV, you'll note several additional sections that aren't included in resumes for the private sector: *Publications, Teaching Experience, Grants and Awards*, and *Presentations*. You'll also note that education CVs generally lead with the Education section, much like legal and medical resumes.

### In Summary

Regardless of the industry you're in or the format you choose for your resume / CV, the principles I have presented through the chapters in this book have equal applicability. You must tailor your resume to every job for which you apply – one size really does not fit all. You

> **Regardless of the industry, the same principles apply to resumes!**

must list accomplishments to showcase your excellence. Your resume must be perfect – no typos or grammar problems; this used to be enough to make you stand out…it is the bare minimum requirement now – almost everyone will meet this standard.

### Resume Samples checklist

_____ Regardless of industry or format, resumes follow the same principles.

_____ Select a resume format that is appealing to you and to hiring managers.

_____ Be willing to try several different resume formats and styles to determine which is best for you. **REMEMBER: TWO PAGES MAXIMUM!**

_____ Regardless of the industry, you must tailor your resume.

_____ Military to private industry transition – watch the acronyms and jargon.

_____ Education / academia resumes are called Curriculum Vitae (CVs).

---

**Note**: the sample resumes discussed in this chapter appear on the following pages. Some of these resumes are longer than two pages – *which should be your max except for the Educator CV* – but are done so here for presentation purposes only!

- Military resume, pages 126-128
- Gaming resume, pages 128-130
- IT resume, pages 130-132
- HR resume, pages 133-136
- Top Exec resume, pages 136-138
- Educator CV, pages 138-144

---

# Jeffrey L. Blau, Lt. Col. (ret), USMC

Jeff's Address
Jeff's City and Zip Code
Jeff's phone # (h), Jeff's cell # (c)
Jeff's e-mail address

## SUMMARY OF QUALIFICATIONS

Seasoned Public Affairs professional with a wide breadth and depth of public affairs and strategic communication experience. Comprehensive understanding and record of implementing communication principles and strategies. Currently a Senior Military Analyst specializing in providing open source information and media analysis products relevant to U.S. Pacific Command (USPACOM) issues. Ability to recognize and mitigate potentially negative public relations situations. Exceptional track record in planning and executing Public Affairs plans and strategies under a variety of demanding situations. Strengths include:

- Crisis / Strategic Communication
- Planning / Executing PA Strategies
- Crafting Public Affairs Messages
- Developing Relationships with Media Reps
- Gauging Regional Reaction

- Media Analysis / Assessment
- Inter-Agency Coordination
- Facilitating Table-Top Exercises
- Asia Pacific Regional Expertise
- Talking Point / Speech Preparation

## PROFESSIONAL EXPERIENCE

**Cubic Applications Inc. supporting USPACOM J7, Honolulu, HI     2010 to Present
Senior Military Analyst**

- Site representative at Pacific Warfighting Center for Cubic Applications Inc. Responsible for all HR functions and task supervision of 15-17 individuals on a daily basis. Successfully resolved all HR issues that arose.

- Support the planning / execution of U.S. Pacific Command (USPACOM) exercises throughout the Asia Pacific region. Facilitated small group, focused problem-solving discussions by senior civilian and military leaders of allied and partner nations. Efforts built much-needed relationship bridges between civilian and military leaders.

- Analyst and contributing member of USPACOM's Media Analysis and Productions (MAP) team that provided tailored open-source information and media analysis products on relevant USPACOM issues. Created a daily media summary with analysis for senior USPACOM leaders and Strategic Focus Groups. Hailed as superior quality by senior military leaders.

**U.S. Marine Corps Forces Pacific, Camp H.M. Smith, HI          2004 to 2010
Director of Public Affairs**

- Coordinated the Public Affairs activities at 17 bases and stations throughout the Marine Forces Pacific Area of Operations. Responsible for the planning and execution of PA engagement for exercises and contingencies, keeping all organizations and agencies abreast of developments so coordination could be complete and effective.

• Routinely coordinated MARFORPAC PA activities with State Department personnel at U.S. Embassies throughout the Asia / Pacific region.

• Directly supported commander and senior staff in all facets of Public Affairs activities including: acting as spokesperson, preparing for and facilitating interviews, creating talking points, strategic messages and identifying opportunities for engagement. All activities completed on time with no technical difficulties.

**III Marine Expeditionary Force, Okinawa, Japan**       **2001 to 2004**
**Director of Public Affairs**

• Directed a staff of 25+ Marines, civilians, and Japanese national workers who co-ordinated and executed all Public Affairs activities on Okinawa, and throughout the IIIMEF / Marine Corps Bases Japan area. All efforts coordinated successfully between US and Japanese participants.

• Coordinated the Public Affairs response and engagement for numerous serious and politically sensitive incidents involving Marines and family members such as: aircraft incidents, sexual assault, arson, theft and environmental mishaps. Difficult, emotionally volatile situations defused with professionalism, diplomacy and tact.

• Developed and published groundbreaking bi-lingual English / Japanese language magazine designed to improve the image of U.S. military and family members within the Okinawan community. Magazine was extremely effective in circumventing local media's anti-U.S. bias, by communicating the US message directly to Okinawan neighbors.

**U.S. Central Command, Tampa, FL**       **1998 to 2001**
**Public Affairs Plans Officer**

• Routinely participated as the Public Affairs representative to the Strategic Communication and Information Operations working groups. Extremely familiar with the Military Decision Making Process (MDMP).

• Deployed multiple times to Egypt to execute PA activities supporting exercise Bright Star involving multiple countries and media from all over the Middle East.

**2nd Marine Aircraft Wing, Marine Corps Bases East, Havelock NC**       **1995 to 1998**
**Director of Public Affairs**

• Led the Public Affairs element in Aviano, Italy supporting the accident investigation team for a Marine aircraft that cut a suspension cable for a ski gondola, resulting in the deaths of 20 European civilians. This international incident involved dozens of media outlets. Coordinated all media events for the release and public briefing of investigation results.

• Managed all Public Affairs activities for the Marine Corps Air Station and Aircraft Wing including interaction and liaison with local community leaders of Havelock,

NC. Routinely and successfully handled sensitive issues such as property encroachment surrounding the base, environmental concerns and noise complaints.

• Effectively mitigated crisis situations involving four separate events where Marine aircraft crashed resulting in death and property losses. Able to smooth over emotionally charged situations.

---

## EDUCATION

**Masters of General Administration / Marketing, University of Maryland University College** (Adelphi, Maryland)

**Bachelor of Science Operations / Production Management**, Arizona State University (Tempe, Arizona)

---

## MEMBERSHIPS / SECURITY CLEARANCE

Long-time member of the Public Relations Society of America

Current Top Secret / Sensitive Compartmented Information (TS/SCI), completed periodic reinvestigation June 2010

Eagle Scout

# William Michaels
His street, city, state and zip code
His phone # and e-mail address

---

### Summary of Qualifications

Skilled table games dealer with a record of outstanding customer service. Experienced in a wide variety of table games, and interfacing with the public. Game and casino protection and customer service are my focus.

### Areas of Gaming Expertise

| | | |
|---|---|---|
| • Craps | • Three-card Poker | • Blackjack |
| • Texas Holdem | • Let It Ride | • Roulette (learning) |
| • All Carnival Games | • Mississippi Stud | • Pai Gow (learning) |

# RESUME SAMPLES

---

**Professional Experience**

---

### Table Games Dealer                                   April 2011 to Present
Caesars Entertainment, Paris / Bally's Hotel and Casino, Las Vegas, NV

- Effectively provided a wide range of gaming experiences for my customers, including Craps, Blackjack (single deck, two deck and shoe), Three Card Poker, Let it Ride and most Carnival games, Mississippi Stud, Crazy 4, and Texas Holdem.

- Breadth and knowledge of a wide range of games provides floor supervisor and shift manager greater flexibility in scheduling game coverage at the casino.

- Provide exceptional game and casino protection, protecting the integrity of the game and the casino.

- Rated as Role Model employee due to excellence in performance and customer service.

### Craps Dealer                                         January 2011 to April 2011
Golden Gate Casino, Las Vegas, NV

- Effectively provided gaming entertainment for Craps players at the casino, ensuring that players had the best experience possible.

- Responsible for having a complete knowledge of the game of Craps, and its proper payouts and procedures.

- Provided exceptional game and casino protection, protecting the integrity of the game and the casino.

### Server and Bartender                                 March 2002 to December 2010
Outback Steakhouse, Colorado Springs, CO and Las Vegas, NV

- Provided exceptional customer service to diners. Abilities were recognized by being named "Head Wait," a position of responsibility few held. Responsibilities included handling, accounting for and depositing large sums of money each night.

- Responsible for preparing and serving a wide range of alcoholic beverages and knowing their composition. A major responsibility was ensuring that all customers were old enough to purchase alcohol, and watching for those who had too much to drink.

- Complete knowledge of menu items and liquor options allowed me to provide outstanding customer service to diners – making entrée or dessert recommendations, drink recommendations, etc.

### Server                                               April 1996 to March 2002
Old Chicago, Colorado Springs, CO

- Provided exceptional customer service to diners. This included working off-site events, in particular for special needs children, sporting events, and fund raisers. Positive interaction with the community was a necessity.

**129**

• Complete knowledge of menu items and liquor options allowed me to provide outstanding customer service to diners – making entrée or dessert recommendations, drink recommendations, etc.

---

**Education**

**Nick Kallos Casino Gaming School – Craps procedures and proper payouts**
Las Vegas, Nevada

**Pikes Peak Community College, Business (four semesters completed)**
Colorado Springs, Colorado

---

**References**

**Bob Jones** – Outback Steakhouse (Manager), (telephone # and e-mail address)

**Larry Smith** – Outback Steakhouse (Owner) – (telephone # and e-mail address)

**Henry Brown** – Old Chicago (Manager) – (telephone # and e-mail address)

---

## IT Pro

| Street address, city, state zip code | Cell phone # | e-mail@gmail.com |

---

Detail-oriented, innovative senior IT professional with exceptional desktop and system administration skills. Nearly two decades of progressively more responsible desktop support, system and network administration experience in several industries.

| **Key Strengths and Technical Competencies** | Windows XP, Windows 7 and 8 configuration, maintenance and support, MS IIS web server support, MS SQL server configuration and support, Sharepoint, Microsoft Windows Server 2000, 2003, 2008 and 2012 configuration and management. Active Directory management. Troubleshooting, network administration, problem solving, system analysis and project management. |

---

**PROFESSIONAL EXPERIENCE**

**Senior Systems Administrator,**                                    **2002 to Present**
Ace Right Electronics, Commerce City, CO

- (Promoted three times) Served as Systems administrator for a very active and sophisticated user group. Exceeded internal client expectations by providing 99.7% up time over the course of the last five years. Two years in the past ten had zero downtime due to system errors or disruptions.

- Project managed software upgrades from XP to Windows 7 and Windows 7 to Windows 8. Prior to implementation, advised and trained users on new features and what to expect from the new software platforms. Upgrades performed under budget and ahead of schedule.

- Used creative problem solving and analytical skills to isolate and repair an issue with our network that threatened to disrupt users. Out-of-hours work resulted in problem identification, isolation and repair. Users were never aware a problem existed.

- Configured, constructed and maintained user workstations for a technically adept user community. Determined how to support customized computer applications for users who needed something different than what the corporate software template was.

- Led the development and implementation of an in-house trouble ticket system designed to allow users to report outages or computer difficulties, and allowed system technicians to share knowledge about fixes and patches that worked. Once system was up and functional, response and repair time was reduced by 43%.

- Provided Tier 1 Network Support to the organization. Troubleshooting addressed such issues as remote access, wireless connectivity for internal and external customers, remote assistance, Windows update issues, Microsoft operating system issues. Provided top-level support, often being able to fix issues before they became widespread problems.

**Systems Administrator**                                           **1995 to 2002**
Argus Conventions

- Principal system administrator responsible for the configuration, installation and maintenance of Microsoft Exchange Server that provided service to 2,000 users in a 24/7 operations environment.  Servers worked smoothly during entire five-year tenure, providing reliable service to all users.

- Desktop support responsibilities included configuring, installing, supporting, and maintaining Windows XP and Windows 7, and effective and proactive support of the Microsoft Office Suite of applications. Support included monthly lunch-and-learns to help end users get the most out of the software applications they were using.

• Used exceptional trouble-shooting skills to diagnose end-user system issues and minimized downtime for users. Diagnosed peripheral device failures and implemented solutions that allowed end users to continue working with a minimum of downtime.

• Configured and led the installation of the company's first Microsoft Exchange Server 2000. Developed and delivered training to over 300 end users to assist them in learning this new application.

## HONORS

Recognized as IT Professional of the Year (selected from over seventy peers) (2006)

Awarded IT Professional of the Quarter three times (2004, 2007 and 2010)

Earned Top Technical Customer Service Award for 2001

## KEY CERTIFICATIONS

Cisco Certified Network Associate (CCNA) Routing and Switching  Certification

Cisco Certified Entry Networking Technician (CCENT) Certification

CompTIA A+ Certified Professional

CompTIA Network Plus certification

Microsoft Certified Systems Administrator (MCSA) Certification

## EDUCATION

Bachelors of Science in Computer Science, major in Network Engineering
University of Colorado at Denver

# W. DANIEL QUILLEN, SPHR

Dan's LinkedIn Profile

---

## SUMMARY OF QUALIFICATIONS

---

Senior Human Resource professional with a record of documented achievement and measurable performance in various industries. Strategic leader committed to providing best-in-class Human Resources support. Seasoned leader with impeccable ethics and integrity. Strengths include:

| | | |
|---|---|---|
| • Legal Compliance | • Succession Planning | • Organizational Development |
| • Talent Acquisition | • Employee Development | • Strategic HR |
| • Employee Relations | • Policy & Procedure Development | • Benefits |

---

## PROFESSIONAL EXPERIENCE

---

**Director of Internal Services**                              **January 2013 to present**
City of Aurora, CO

- Promoted to Director of Internal Services – responsible for management and direction of Human Resources, Risk Management, Purchasing and Fleet Operations for the City of Aurora. (This position is equivalent to Director or Vice President of Administration in the private sector.)

- Part of a small team responsible for developing and implementing a broad succession planning program at the city. Results included the attraction and retention of superior employees.

- Led the effort to replace the compensation and job classification structure for all city positions. Established market pay for employees across all positions at the City, ensuring the ability to recruit and retain employees and to pay them competitive market salaries.

**Division Manager of Human Resources**          **November 2011 to January 2013**
City of Aurora, Colorado

- Effectively managed Employment & Compensation, Benefits, Recruiting and Training teams for the City of Aurora and its 3,700 employees, including 1,000 seasonal / temporary workers.

• Introduced new recruiting strategies and tactics that effectively lowered the response time to our internal customers and candidates.

• Led the performance management program for the city, directing the efforts of managers across the city, ensuring all employees received performance reviews and appropriate pay treatment.

### Director of Human Resources                                       August 2001 to August 2011
Holme Roberts & Owen LLP, Denver, CO

• Protected the firm from lawsuits by handling all disciplinary actions up to and including terminations using sound employment law practices.  Over the course of ten years and 200+ terminations, there were no lawsuits filed against the firm for employment actions.

• Frequent changes within the firm required effective employee relations and interpersonal skills.  Mergers, acquisitions, and recession-related changes in firm policy and guidelines all required extensive ability to inspire and retain employees.  As demonstration of success in these areas, one retiring employee observed, *"Dan put the human back in Human Resources."*

• Effectively managed all health benefits for the firm.  Over a 5-year period, negotiated over $2,000,000 in savings while maintaining one of the best benefits packages in the industry.

• Developed and revised many Human Resources processes and procedures, including performance management, employee development / training curricula and programs, paid leave / PTO, sabbatical, maternity and paternity leave, etc.  This effort provided competitive and attractive policies and procedures allowing the firm to attract and retain top talent.

### Senior Human Resources Manager                                            1998 to 2001
Avaya / Lucent Technologies, Westminster, CO

• Due to success in complex HR situations, was asked to provide HR support to 1,400 Avaya Labs (formerly Bell Labs) scientists, a large department with significant complexity to their HR work (organizational development, recruiting, retention, compensation, etc.).  Earned *Exceeded* and *Far Exceeded* ratings and performance bonuses for work with this group.

• Designed and implemented an organization-wide learning curriculum for managers. Resulting programs identified competency gaps and provided customized learning curricula for managers. Efforts hailed by company executives as breakthrough, creative and highly efficient.

**Human Resources Generalist**                                  **1992 to 1998**
Lucent Technologies / AT&T, Greenwood Village, CO

- Certified as a Competency Consultant. Because of success in this area, was asked to work with a small team to introduce competency modeling company-wide (32,000 employees), including international locations.

- Led the international HR effort of the organization, including working effectively with the employment laws for Ireland, England, Germany, Singapore, Hong Kong, Tokyo and Australia. Was successful in this effort, protecting the company and making sure hiring, performance management and compensation practices met the requirements of the international communities.

## AWARDS / HONORS

- "Dan communicates very well; he knows when to talk and write like an employment lawyer, and when to talk and write like a Director of Human Resources." (Written comment in performance review by an employment law partner with whom I worked extensively.)

- Participant in "fast track" program for executives who exhibit extraordinary leadership potential. (Fewer than 2% of AT&T's employees are given this opportunity.)

- Freelance author. Sixteen books and several articles in national magazines published.

- Consistently rated *Exceeds* or *Far Exceeds* during performance management meetings.

## EDUCATION

**Master of Business Administration, with Human Resource specialization**
Concordia University Wisconsin (Mequon, Wisconsin)

**Bachelor of Science in Business Administration, with Marketing minor**
Thomas Edison State College (Trenton, New Jersey)

---

## CERTIFICATIONS

---

**Certified as Senior Professional in Human Resources (SPHR)**, Society for Human Resource Management.

**Certified as Competency Consultant** (McLagan Process)

# Tom Top
# Executive

Street Address
City, state & zip code
E-mail: address
Cell phone #

Senior executive with a record of documented achievement and measurable performance in diverse industries. Strategic leader committed to organizational change. Community leader with impeccable ethics and integrity.

## CORE COMPETENCIES

- Change Management
- Business Operations
- Strategic Planning
- Influencing Skills

- Team Building
- HR Management
- Marketing
- Public Relations

- Benefits
- Community Outreach
- Process Improvement
- Conflict Management

## PROFESSIONAL EXPERIENCE

### CHIEF EXECUTIVE OFFICER                                          2000 to Present
Aces Electronics – Denver, CO

Reported directly to and accountable to Board of Directors. Responsible for the overall business and financial management of a two-year0old electronics company. Took over the reins of this struggling start up, and weathered two Recessions. The company not only survived during this time, but it thrived. Revenues quintupled in the past fourteen years with double-digit improvement year over year for each of those fourteen years. Took the company public, and returned significant profits for the company's investors and key stakeholders. Responsibilities included strategic planning, business plan development and implementation, focused and visionary leadership, change management and drive for success.

## Selected Successes:

**Financial Management and Forecasting**

**Process Efficiencies & Expense Reduction**

Took struggling start-up from Chapter 11 to a $500 million dollar industry leader in less than a decade.

Increased profits per employee year over year while at the same time providing employment for an increasing number of employees through the years. Initial employee count of 112 now over 900.

**Process Improvements & Earnings Increase**

Maximized the company's earnings while at the same time introducing and driving key efficiencies across the width and breadth of the company. Implemented stringent business processes and procedures.

**Strategic Planning**

Initiated and supported a business-oriented strategic planning process, working with and through company leadership to identify time-bound and measurable goals targeted to a broad strategic plan.

**Brand Marketing**

Established Aces brand as the top in this market segment.

## CHIEF OPERATING OFFICER                                          1996 to 2000
Mountain Toys – Silverthorne, CO

Responsible for the guidance, direction and management of all organizational aspects of this niche recreation company. Established the company's brand and wrested market share from traditional and entrenched market leaders. Took start-up from fifteenth to third in our industry in just over three years second is just around the corner.

## Selected Successes:

**Operational Efficiencies**

Streamlined manufacturing processes, integrating off-shore parts and supplies into just-in-time delivery to maximize our internal and external resources. Shortened product to market cycle by 50% while decreasing defect rate to near zero.

**Financial Leadership and Guidance**

Orchestrated creative financing by partnering with local and national lenders to bring new product to the market six months earlier than expected. Prepared company for IPO. Led financial and strategic analysis of Business Process Outsourcing, ROI analysis and strategic business plan for expanding the company's market.

**Change Management and Strategic Visioning**

Created a vision in company's employees for the future of the company and product line. Empowered employees to recommend changes and improvements to products. Employees responded with enthusiasm. Launched re-branding initiatives for two subsidiaries of the company. Increased media hits over 300% in a two-year period.

| | |
|---|---|
| **Sales Management and Leadership** | Maximized sales budget and expanded markets, engaging retail partners as well as wholesale distributors in an aggressive move to win market share. Sales and marketing strategies increased sales 180%, 220% and 126% over three consecutive years. |
| **Team Building** | Led the merger of two competitive companies with diverse cultures. Helped create one corporate identity that members of both former companies embraced and identified with. |

## **PREVIOUS PROFESSIONAL EXPERIENCE AVAILABLE UPON REQUEST**

## AWARDS AND HONORS

**Entrepreneur of the Year, Summit County, CO 1998**

**President, Leadership Institute (Corporate Think Tank), Denver, CO 2002 to 2005**

## EDUCATION

**M.B.A., Economics**
University of Colorado, Boulder, CO

**B.S., Business Administration**
Statistics and Marketing
University of Colorado, Boulder, CO

## *CURRICULUM VITAE*

# Robert J. Educator, PH.D

State University
His city, state & zip code
His telephone number and His e-mail address

## EDUCATION

• **Ph.D in Spanish and Portuguese**, University of New Mexico, 1999

    o Dissertation: *Hiatus Resolution in Spanish: Phonetic Aspects and Phonological Implications in Northern New Mexico.* Director: D. Rector

- **Master of Arts in Spanish**, University of New Mexico, 1996

- **Bachelor of Arts, Spanish / Political Science**, Public University, 1993

- **Languages**:

  o English: Native

  o Spanish: Superior

  o Portuguese: Advanced

  o French: Intermediate

  o Latin: Grammatical knowledge

## PROFESSIONAL EXPERIENCE

**Chair, Department of Modern Languages**　　　　　　　**January 2011 to Present**
University of _____

**Associate Professor of Spanish, Specialist in Spanish linguistics**　　　**2009 to 2011**
University of _____. Specialist in Spanish linguistics

**Assistant Professor of Spanish**　　　　　　　　　　**1999 to 2001**
University of _____

**Teaching Assistant / Associate**　　　　　　　　　　**1995 to 1999**
University of _____

## REFEREED PUBLICATIONS

2014 (to appear). *Review of Spanish as a Heritage Language in the United States: The State of the Field*. Beaudrie, Sara M. and Marta Fairclough, eds. *Hispania* 97.1.

2013 "El suroeste creciente: Un breve análisis sociodemográfico de la población hispanohablante de los Estados Unidos." In *El español en los Estados Unidos: E Pluribus Unum? Enfoques Multidisciplinarios*, Domnita Dumitrescu and Gerardo Piña-Rosales, eds. Madrid/New York: Academia Norteamericana de la Lengua Española. 31-45.

2010 "The State(s) of Spanish in the Southwest: A Comparative Study of Language Maintenance and Socioeconomic Variables." In *Spanish of the Southwest: A language of transition,* Susana Rivera-Mills and Daniel Villa, eds. Madrid: Iberoamericana, 133-56.

2009 "As the Southwest Moves North: Population Expansion and Sociolinguistic Implications in the Spanish-speaking Southwest." *Southwest Journal of Linguistics*, 28.1: 53-69.

2009   "The Cost of Linguistic Loyalty: Socioeconomic Factors in the Face of Shifting Demographic Trends Among Spanish Speakers in the Southwest." *Spanish in Context* 6.1: 7-25.

2005 (with M. Lockley).  "Interview with Dolf Seilacher." *Ichnos* 12.3: 233-239.

2003  "Bilingual Verb Constructions in Southwest Spanish." *The Bilingual Review/La Revista Bilingüe*, 27.3: 195-204.

---

## COURSES TAUGHT

SPAN 1011   Intensive Beginning Spanish (2003)

SPAN 2110   Intermediate Spanish I (2003, 2004)

SPAN 3010   Advanced Conversation & Composition I (2001, 2002, 2003, 2004)

SPAN 3020   Advanced Conversation & Composition II (2003, 2004, 2005, 2006, 2007, 2009)

SPAN 3060   Spanish Phonetics (2002, 2003, 2004, 2005, 2006, 2007, 2008, 2009)

SPAN 3070   Bilingual Communities: Spanish as a Language of Contact (2001, '03, '05, '07, '10, '13)

*SPAN 3225   Special Topics in Hispanic Culture: El Béisbol (2013)

SPAN 3310   Advanced Grammar & Writing (2007, 2008)

SPAN 1011   Intensive Beginning Spanish (2003)

SPAN 2110   Intermediate Spanish I (2003, 2004)

SPAN 3010   Advanced Conversation & Composition I (2001, 2002, 2003, 2004)

SPAN 3020   Advanced Conversation & Composition II (2003, 2004, 2005, 2006, 2007, 2009)

SPAN 3060   Spanish Phonetics (2002, 2003, 2004, 2005, 2006, 2007, 2008, 2009)

SPAN 3070   Bilingual Communities: Spanish as a Language of Contact (2001, '03, '05, '07, '10, '13)

*SPAN 3225   Special Topics in Hispanic Culture: El Béisbol (2013)

SPAN 3310   Advanced Grammar & Writing (2007, 2008)

SPAN 4010/5010   History of the Spanish Language (2002, 2006, 2008, 2011)

*SPAN 4020/5020   Spanish Sociolinguistics (2006, 2007, 2009, 2012)

*SPAN 4020/5020      Spanish Sociolinguistics (2006, 2007, 2009, 2012)

*SPAN 4060/5060      Dialects of the Spanish-speaking World (2004, 2006, 2008, 2010, 2013)

*SPAN 4076/5076      Spanish in a Western State (2009, 2011, 2012)

*SPAN 4080/5980      Spanish in the United States (2007, 2009, 2011)

*SPAN 4970/5970      ST: Advanced Spanish Grammar (2002)

*MLNG 4690/5690      Methods of Teaching Modern Languages (2004, 2005)

*Denotes courses that I proposed, created and added to the University curriculum

## PRESENTATIONS AT PROFESSIONAL MEETINGS

"Spanish on the map: Population growth and Spanish-language maintenance in the United States." *24th Conference on Spanish in the United States and 9th International Conference on Spanish in Contact with Other Languages in the Ibero-American World. March 6-9, 2013. McAllen, TX.*

"Language Shift and shifting borders: Spanish language maintenance and distance from the Mexican border in the Southwest." *The 41st Annual Meeting of the Linguistic Association of the Southwest.* October 11-13, 2012. Ft. Wayne, IN

"Más allá del Mississippi: Demographic change and scholarly shift in the Spanish-speaking Southwest." **Presidential address**. *The 39th Annual Meeting of the Linguistic Association of the Southwest.* October 7-9, 2010. Las Cruces, NM

"El suroeste creciente: La situación sociolingüística en el occidente hispanohablante de los Estados Unidos." *92nd Annual AATSP Conference.* July 10-13, 2010. Guadalajara, México.

"As the Southwest moves north: Population expansion and sociolinguistic implications in the Spanish-speaking Southwest." *The Four Corners Conference on Immigration.* October 9-10, 2009. Grand Junction, CO.

"Spanish in the non-border Southwest." *The 38th Annual Meeting of the Linguistic Association of the Southwest.* September 24-26, 2009. Provo, UT.

"As the Southwest moves north: Population expansion and social implications in the Spanish-speaking Southwest." *42nd Congress of the Southwest Council of Latin American Studies.* March 11-14, 2009. Santo Domingo, Dominican Republic.

"The Southwest moves north: Population expansion and sociolinguistic implications in the Spanish-speaking Southwest." *The 37th Annual Meeting of the Linguistic Association of the Southwest.* October 17-19, 2008. Corvallis, OR.

"Spanish on the map: Population growth and Spanish-language maintenance in the United States." *24th Conference on Spanish in the United States and 9th International Conference on Spanish in Contact with Other Languages in the Ibero-American World.* March 6-9, 2013. McAllen, TX.

"Language Shift and shifting borders: Spanish language maintenance and distance from the Mexican border in the Southwest." *The 41st Annual Meeting of the Linguistic Association of the Southwest.* October 11-13, 2012. Ft. Wayne, IN

"Más allá del Mississippi: Demographic change and scholarly shift in the Spanish-speaking Southwest." **Presidential address**. *The 39th Annual Meeting of the Linguistic Association of the Southwest.* October 7-9, 2010. Las Cruces, NM

"El suroeste creciente: La situación sociolingüística en el occidente hispanohablante de los Estados Unidos." *92nd Annual AATSP Conference.* July 10-13, 2010. Guadalajara, México.

"As the Southwest moves north: Population expansion and sociolinguistic implications in the Spanish-speaking Southwest." *The Four Corners Conference on Immigration.* October 9-10, 2009. Grand Junction, CO.

"Spanish in the non-border Southwest." *The 38th Annual Meeting of the Linguistic Association of the Southwest.* September 24-26, 2009. Provo, UT.

"As the Southwest moves north: Population expansion and social implications in the Spanish-speaking Southwest." *42nd Congress of the Southwest Council of Latin American Studies.* March 11-14, 2009. Santo Domingo, Dominican Republic.

"The Southwest moves north: Population expansion and sociolinguistic implications in the Spanish-speaking Southwest." *The 37th Annual Meeting of the Linguistic Association of the Southwest.* October 17-19, 2008. Corvallis, OR.
**Invited Speaker** (two 3-hour sessions) for University of Northern Colorado M.A. Pedagogy Week. June 10-11, 2008. Topics: Sociolinguistics and bilingualism. Greeley, CO.

"Redrawing the map: Population expansion and sociolinguistic implications in the Spanish-speaking Southwest." *Hispanic Linguistics Symposium 2007.* November 1-4, 2007. San Antonio, Texas.

"The state(s) of Spanish in the Southwest: A comparative analysis." *The 35th Annual Meeting of the Linguistic Association of the Southwest.* September 29-October 1, 2006. Laredo, TX.

"As the Southwest moves north: Population expansion and sociolinguistic implications in the Spanish-speaking Southwest." *The Four Corners Conference on Immigration.* October 9-10, 2009. Grand Junction, CO.

## AWARDS AND GRANTS

2013 CLAS ACT (Advancing Curriculum and Teaching) Grant. **$2050** to develop Spanish for Heritage Speakers program.

2009 **CLAS Award for Excellence in Teaching**. Public University College of Liberal Arts and Sciences.

2009 **CLAS Award for Excellence in Service**. Public University College of Liberal Arts and Sciences.

2007 Public University Modern Languages Department **$1000** for LASSO conference.

2007 Another University Spanish and Portuguese Department **$500** for LASSO conference.

2006 President's Fund for the Humanities Grant. **$3394**. "Linguistic Legacies: The 36th Annual Meeting of the Linguistic Association of the Southwest (LASSO)." Funding to host the annual LASSO conference at Public Universiy in September 2007.

2005 YUMPs award. **$400** to support travel to conference (Lubbock, TX).

2005 **CLAS Award for Excellence in Teaching**. Public University College of Liberal Arts and Sciences.

2005 Faculty Development Grant. **$500** (to purchase mapping software) "Spanish language use in the Southwest United States."

2004 Faculty Development Grant. **$5000** to develop hybrid Methods of Teaching Modern Languages course.

## PROFESSIONAL MEMBERSHIPS

Linguistic Association of the Southwest (LASSO) – Lifetime member

Modern Language Association (MLA)

American Association of Teachers of Spanish and Portuguese (AATSP)

## SELECTED OTHER PROFESSIONAL ACTIVITIES

2012-present **Learning Enhancement Task Force**, College of Liberal Arts & Sciences (CLAS)

2011-present **Commencement Reader**—Serve on the Commencement Steering Committee and read the names of the graduates at Public University graduation ceremonies (fall and spring).

2011-present **Spanish Lower-Division Coordinator**—All of the coordination of the lower-division program, including coordination of the Succeed Concurrent Enrollment program.

2010-present **Post-Tenure Review Committee**, CLAS

These resume samples will put me on the right path!

## 14   Letters of Recommendation

*You don't carry in your countenance a letter of recommendation.*
Charles Dickens

Letters of recommendation are often overlooked but important arrows in your job-search quiver, and are resources you should consider using to assist in your job search.

I have found that letters of recommendation work best when they are written by former managers for whom you worked. You may be wondering how you go about procuring such instruments to use in your job hunt. The answer is simple: Just ask. When I was laid off from my job at a large western law firm, my boss – the Chief Operating Officer – was also laid off, as were five of my peers. The decision had nothing to do with our skills, abilities or competence – it was merely a business decision, driven by the need to shed salaries so our firm would look more attractive to potential suitors, who might be willing to merge with / absorb our firm.

As soon as I knew I had been laid off, I asked my boss to provide me a letter of recommendation on firm letter head. I also reached out to the former COO who had hired me into the position, and for whom I had worked for my first seven years at the firm, and asked him if he would be willing to provide me with a letter of recommendation as well. Both my boss and my former boss agreed – sort of.

The *sort of* part was this: while both were willing to provide me with letters of recommendation, each one asked that I provide them a draft of what I was looking for, and they would then add their two cents' worth. I have since learned that this is a very common practice with higher-level executives.

That sounded fair to me – I knew what I wanted the letters to say. I wanted the letters to address some of the major accomplishments I had achieved while working for the firm, because I thought they would be major selling points for potential hiring managers.

But I'll be honest – I was a little nervous about doing it; however, I felt the letters would be worth my effort. I didn't want to present a letter to either of my former bosses that might make them feel uncomfortable, but I also needed the letters to be very factual and positive. I decided upon a tactic that worked well for me, and which seemed to work well for both my bosses. Perhaps you will find it worthwhile if you find yourself in the same position.

To come up with statements I knew each person would be supportive of, I went back through my previous years' performance evaluations, and gleaned positive comments my managers had made about me. I then crafted them around the major professional accomplishments I had made to the firm.

Once the letters were created, I provided them to my former managers, and asked them to write their versions on their firm's letterhead. I also let them know what I had done – that I had gone back through my performance evaluations and used their own language whenever possible.

Following is a transcription of the letter of recommendation I received from one of my former managers:

# LETTERS OF RECOMMENDATION

June 9, 2011

Re: Dan Quillen

Dear Hiring Manager:

In the legal services industry, conventional wisdom is that when you are filling a critical and sensitive role such as Director of Human Resources, the candidate you select should have relevant law firm experience. When Dan Quillen interviewed for the role at HRO, I saw in Dan qualities and attributes I felt would make him an excellent Director of Human Resources for our firm, despite his lack of direct experience with law firms.

Dan worked hard to learn the nuances and differences of the legal services industry and to adapt his professional background and experience to the law firm culture. He acknowledged key stakeholders and worked well with individuals at all levels within the firm.

Dan proved to be an excellent Director of Human Resources for our firm. He demonstrated calm and professional judgment in fulfilling his responsibilities. Human relations and all that revolves around these elements of his role can be sensitive and volatile at times, and included in Dan's strengths are his demeanor and approach to such instances.

In addition to his skills in employee relations, Dan worked at becoming an expert on our benefits plans. This was not an area of focus for him with his previous employers. His efforts in this regard allowed him to negotiate successfully with our carriers, resulting in significant savings for our firm. Over one three-year period, these savings surpassed over $1,000,000.

One of Dan's main responsibilities was to help protect the firm from lawsuits for employment-related issues. During his ten years with the firm, Dan was responsible for the termination of over 200 individuals. Yet, despite the fact that individuals in law firms can often be more litigious by nature than the rest of the population, not one lawsuit was filed against the firm for employment-related actions. This was of inestimable value to the firm. One of the employment law partners with whom Dan worked closely observed in her written performance review for him: "Dan communicates very well, he knows when to talk and write like an employment lawyer, and when to talk and write like an HR Director."

Because Dan's skill set extended beyond human resources, we were able to ask him to fill the role of Director of Legal Recruiting on an interim basis when that Director left the firm. While continuing with his HR Director role, Dan was able to step up and fulfill the responsibilities associated with this additional role for 18 months until we could find a suitable candidate to fill this role. Dan's efforts in this regard saved the firm over $200,000 during this period.

Dan enjoyed the respect of lawyers, staff and his colleagues on the senior management team. I can recommend him for any senior HR position you may have for which he has the skills and experience you are seeking. If you have any questions, please contact me at _____ or (e-mail address).

Very truly yours,

Stephen G. Blackwell
Chief Operating Officer

**Be sure to get and use letters of recommendation**

The most powerful letters of recommendation come from former managers. Close behind are letters from customers. Letters of recommendation from former co-workers, peers and direct reports are good, but not as good as those written by former managers.

You should use your letters of recommendation whenever you are putting together an applications packet. When you are uploading your resume and cover letter into applications software, include your letters of recommendation. When you are e-mailing your resume and cover letter to a hiring manager, be sure to include your letters of recommendation.

Letters of recommendation are powerful tools that you should consider an important part of your job search arsenal.

# LETTERS OF RECOMMENDATION

**Letters of Recommendation checklist**

_____ Letters of recommendation can be powerful assists in your job search.

_____ Don't be afraid to ask for a letter of recommendation from a boss, co-worker, peer or someone who works for you.

_____ You may need to suggest things you would like for them to put in your letter of recommendation.

_____ Sometimes, the person you ask for a letter of recommendation may ask you to write it for their signature (good deal!).

_____ Use your letters of recommendation whenever you put together an application packet.

**15** Baker's Dozen of Resume Errors

*When in doubt tell the truth.*
Mark Twain

By now, you should have a pretty good feeling about the basics of resume writing – no typos, grammar difficulties, crisp and professional look and feel, plenty of white space, etc., etc. Let me provide a summary of a few things you should keep in mind while you are assembling your resume. Below is a Baker's Dozen (plus a few more, actually!) of resume errors I see often that you should avoid.

Here is the list of resume forbidden elements:

**Be honest**. I have reviewed resumes that contradicted themselves between entries or between the resume and the cover letter. Your *Summary* statement says you have ten years accounting experience? When I add up the experience at your various jobs as listed on your resume, they only come to a little over seven years. Rounding up from seven to ten isn't Kosher. I am always particularly concerned when I interview a candidate and what they tell me doesn't match with what they said in their resume. As my mother used to teach me – the Truth never changes, and is easier to remember than a lie.

**Don't puff**. (No, I'm not referring to President Clinton's assertion that he 'didn't inhale' when asked if he'd ever smoked marijuana!) Don't pretend you were more than you were in your previous jobs. I once hired a woman who interviewed well and looked great on her resume – she had all the right credentials, had done many of the things we needed done on the job, etc. We had very high hopes and expectations when we brought her in.

Because of her experience and background, we simply handed her large projects and said, "Go get 'im, Tiger." She failed miserably! She didn't have the first clue about how to do the job. Upon further investigation with her, she admitted she hadn't really led those large projects she cited on her resume – she helped out. She had a small part in them. Someone else had been the leader; she just carried out the instructions she was given. All of this became apparent when she was handed the baton and told to run with our projects.

The good news is that she got the job. The bad news is that she got fired from the job for incompetence. Don't let that happen to you.

**No typos**. Please understand you cannot afford to have typos in your resumes. Review your resume multiple times, reading slowly and critically. Ask a friend (not a spouse or parent) to review your resume – and ask them for any suggestions at all, even if they think they are minor.

**No grammar difficulties**. Sometimes as you craft your resume, you may add or delete items without changing the rest of the sentence, which in turn causes grammar difficulties. For example, here is an entry from my resume:

> Established national contracts with several recruiters, negotiating a lower rate than was normally offered.

But then I decided to change the sentence a bit to:

> Established national contracts with several recruiters, negotiating lower rates than was normally offered.

Since I changed *rate* to *rates*, I should have changed the word *was* to *were*, since rates should be plural:

> Established national contracts with several recruiters, negotiating lower rates than **were** normally offered.

**Not tailored**. I hope you realize the value and criticality of tailoring your resume for and to every job for which you apply. Thinking of doing otherwise (i.e. – submitting a generic resume to a job) should just give you the creeps.

**Too general**. This item goes hand-in-hand with #6 – sometimes candidates try to be "all things to all people" and they'll submit a very general, broad resume. Instead, they come across as "no things to any people."

**Too busy**. As you craft your resume, be aware of the look and feel it has. Does it look cramped? Have you shrunk the margins at the top, bottom and sides to help you keep your resume to two pages? Does the reader get eye-whiplash looking from one bolded, underlined, italicized and otherwise formatted element of your resume to another? Judicious formatting is good, just don't overload your readers.

**Incorrect contact information**. While it doesn't happen often, I have on occasion reached out to a candidate and their contact information was incorrect – their e-mail address was mis-typed, or their phone number had been disconnected. Sometimes people will change their e-mail addresses because their spam filters have ceased to be effective…but they forget to change the e-mail address on their resume.

**No accomplishments**. You should be homed in on providing accomplishments on your resume, not just a list of tasks and responsibilities you performed on the job. Accomplishments tell your resume reviewers that you are more than a run-of-the-mill candidate.

**Wrong *Objective* Statement**. I mentioned this earlier in the book, and I will mention it again. First off, with me, if you have an *Objective* statement, it's probably wrong anyway, since I don't care for them. But beyond that, I have to smile as I read someone's *Objective* statement that tells me they want to work in the health care industry…when I am not in the health care industry.

**Paragraphs instead of bullet points**. Busy HR departments, recruiters and hiring managers don't have time to read lengthy paragraphs on resumes, looking for experiences that apply to the job they have open. It is best to bulletize your key points, rather than put them in paragraph form. Consider the difference between these two entries, identical except one is in paragraph form, the other is bulletized:

Coordinate the Public Affairs activities at 17 bases and stations throughout the Marine Forces Pacific Area of Operations. Responsible for the planning and execution of PA engagement for exercises and contingencies. Deployed to conduct PA support for Humanitarian Relief operations following a tsunami in Burma. Routinely coordinated MARFORPAC PA activities with State Department personnel at U.S. Embassies throughout the Asia / Pacific region and with our higher headquarters. Directly supported commander and senior staff in all facets of Public Affairs activities including: acting as spokesperson, preparing for and facilitating interviews, creating talking points, strategic messages and identifying opportunities for engagement.

---

• Coordinate the Public Affairs activities at 17 bases and stations throughout the Marine Forces Pacific Area of Operations. Responsible for the planning and execution of PA engagement for exercises and contingencies.

• Deployed to conduct PA support for Humanitarian Relief operations following a tsunami in Burma.

• Routinely coordinated MARFORPAC PA activities with State Department personnel at U.S. Embassies throughout the Asia / Pacific region and with our higher headquarters.

• Directly supported commander and senior staff in all facets of Public Affairs activities including: acting as spokesperson, preparing for and facilitating interviews, creating talking points, strategic messages and identifying opportunities for engagement.

I think they are easier and quicker to read as bullet points, rather than paragraphs.

**Too much information provided for older jobs**. The most relevant jobs are your most current jobs. For jobs you worked ten or fifteen years' ago, you need only enter a couple bullet points, versus twice that for your most current jobs.

**Poor appearance**. We addressed this specifically in the *Appearance Matters* chapter – your resume needs to have a professional look and feel. Some resumes are just flat and uninspiring; even the addition of limited formatting will help them look more professional.

**Too many acronyms**. This is a caution for military men and women in particular, but no industry is immune. Just because you know what an acronym means, and maybe even the hiring manager, the recruiter or HR professional may not. The first time you use an acronym, spell it out, followed by the acronym in parenthesis. Then you can use just the acronym later in your resume. For example: Certified Fraud Examiner (CFE). Make sure the resume screener understands the language you are speaking.

**References available upon request**. I mentioned this earlier, and I will say it again – please don't include this statement. I always assume references are available upon request. It merely takes up space, and doesn't add a thing to your resume. Use the space to tell me again what a great candidate you are by providing one more accomplishment that might catch my eye.

That doesn't mean you can't add your references as part of your resume. Generally, your references should be included on separate page. If that makes your resume three pages, that's okay – I don't really count the *References* page as part of the resume. If you are early in your career, it may be the second page of your resume, or even the last half / third or your second page. That is okay.

**No personal information**. Please don't put personal information on your resume, like your hobbies, spouse's and childrens' names, hobbies, sports teams, etc.

# BAKER'S DOZEN OF RESUME ERRORS

So – there you have it: a quick glance at things you need to pay attention to as you assemble your resume.

**Baker's Dozen of Resume Errors checklist**

**Pay attention to this list!**

_____ Be honest on your resume – don't puff your experiences.

_____ Carefully proofread your resume multiple times.

_____ Tailor your resume to every job.

_____ Make sure your contact information is correct.

_____ Is your resume too acronymical, without spelling out what the acronym stands for at least once, the first time you use it?

_____ Limit the information you provide for older jobs.

_____ Put as many accomplishments in your resume as you can.

_____ Remove your *Objective* statement; don't put *References Available Upon Request* (but it's okay to provide a list of references).

**16** Miscellany

*You miss 100% of the shots you don't take.*
Wayne Gretzky

We've come to the end of this book about resumes. Before finishing off, however, I want to share a few things that don't fit well into any of the previous chapters, but are things I would like to share and are worth your consideration.

**Put it in Gear**

Don't spend so much time creating the perfect resume that you miss out on job opportunities. I am not talking about a couple of hours or even a day or two to tailor your resume – I am talking about taking much longer. I have a couple friends I worked with on their resumes; we got them in pretty good shape, and they were then going to do the final polishing on them. I was stunned to find out that even though we had met several months earlier, and I gave them suggestions on how to sharpen and improve their resumes, they were still working on them, and hadn't applied for any jobs in the interim!  If you don't apply for a job – even if with an imperfect resume – the answer is ALWAYS "No."

 Don't let activity get in the way of *productive* activity. If you spend three days learning about a company you are thinking about applying to, and the job ad closes, you may feel like you have been working to find a job, when in reality you were just doing unproductive busy work.  (It wouldn't be unproductive busy work if you have an upcoming interview with a company and you are researching them for clues about how to make yourself more valuable to them.)

### Moms Going Back to Work

I have had the opportunity of working with a number of women recently who were re-entering the work force after having stayed home to raise children for a decade or more. My counsel to those who find themselves in

> **Tailoring your resume is critical, but don't spend so much time tailoring that the job closes!**

this situation is simple: let the hiring manager / recruiter / HR department know the reason you were out of the work force. Do so either in your cover letter or in your resume. I will tell you that as a hiring manager, I am concerned when I see a decade-long gap in employment. However, the moment I learn it is because they were raising children, the gap automatically disappears for me. But – I have to know.

You can let me know in your summary statement:

> **Accounting professional returning to work after a decade of raising her family...**

as a bolded sentence in your resume:

> **Left the work force to raise a family**

Or in your cover letter:

> **Dear Hiring Manager,**
>
> **After taking ten years off to raise my family, I am re-entering the work-force. As a dedicated accounting professional prior to my sabbatical....**

There may be some concern that your skills have eroded during the intervening years, especially in technical fields. If you are an IT professional, for example, be certain the hiring manager knows what you have been doing to keep your skills up to date during your time off – whether reading trade magazines, attending night or online classes, participating in conferences, etc.

## Felons

For years the Department of Justice has prohibited companies who do background checks to use arrest records as a disqualifier for candidates because arrest records adversely affect minorities. Now they have decided that *conviction* records also adversely affect minorities. So – employers have to make sure the reason for the felony conviction should exclude the candidate from a job. For example, if convicted of embezzlement, I would be okay not to hire someone who would have access to financial records, cash, etc.

But if there is no direct correlation to the job I have open – streets worker, golf maintenance worker, IT professional, etc., etc., then I am not allowed to disqualify a candidate just because s/he has a felony conviction.

While this is not generally being practiced in private industry, it has taken hold in governmental organizations – city, county, state and federal employers are aware of this prohibition and are willing to work with felons.

The construction industry offers many opportunities for ex-felons to work – drywallers, finish carpenters, carpet and tile layers, brick masons, plumbers, electricians, etc., are all opportunities available.

When asked about your gap in employment (the time you were incarcerated), be up front and honest:

> You know, when I was younger, I made some mistakes in judgment and had to spend a little time in prison to pay for my lapse in judgment. I learned a lot during that time and am ready to be a contributing member of society.

If you don't have schooling, go get some! Following is a list of some of the hottest areas for work in the United States. These jobs require associate's degrees:

- Paralegal

- Registered nurse

- Dental hygienist

- Computer programmer

- Medical records technician

I have the opportunity to work with many individuals who are short on experience and schooling. I have looked for opportunities that they could do while they look for something permanent. There are a number of companies / industries that always seem to have high turn-over – a perfect opportunity for you to find work:

- Convenience stores

- Airlines – baggage handlers, reservation agents

- Sales positions in many industries

- Merchandisers – those folks who stock shelves at convenience stores. Check out NARMS (National Association for Retail Marketing Services)

- Drivers in many industries (requires a good driving record)

- Truck drivers (requires a good driving record, CDL)

So if you've mis-stepped, don't dismay – there are options out there that may be just right for you.

**References**

By now you'll expect me to say: Don't put *References Available Upon Request* on your resume. And you're right. But I do have a thought or two about references.

First and foremost – make certain those whom you list as references will give you a positive reference. Through the years, I have been amazed at the things people have told me about candidates for a job I have open. They are less than complimentary, less than impressed with the person, and they're not afraid to tell me so! If you find yourself getting interviews, but after your references are checked you hear nothing, you should consider whether the people you are providing as references are doing you a favor or not.

Before you give someone's name and contact information out as a reference, be sure and ask them if they would be willing to serve as a reference for you. If you sense *any* hesitation whatsoever, you would probably be well-advised to think of someone else to use as a reference.

After you've settled on three or four individuals as references, set about getting their information to provide to hiring managers: their phone number (home, work and cell), e-mail address, their current company and title. Confirm the information with them before providing it to potential hiring companies.

If you provide the name of a person as a reference, you are responsible to have all the correct information! Don't make the person to whom you provide the information about your references have to track them down. I have been astounded at how often I check a reference only to find an e-mail address that bounces back, a phone number that has been disconnected (or has been reassigned to someone else) or the phone number of the company where the person used to work, but they no longer work there.

It's also not very impressive when I call to get a reference on someone and they say, "Who? I'm sorry – I can't recall anyone by that name that has worked for me." (I kid you not – I have heard that more than once by references!)

As mentioned earlier, before you give the name as someone who will serve as a reference for you, be sure you speak with them and get their permission to do so. I have a very close work associate who is particularly good at this. Before he gives my name out, he always checks with me. After he interviews, he calls me and tells me a little about the job, and shares with me what he would like me to say about him. He's not prepping me, per se, but he will let me know what areas he thinks the hiring manager is most interested in. Then he reminds me of his skills and experience in that area. I commend that tactic to you.

**Don't Expect the Company to Work for You!**

Where I work, about once a month our HR department receives an e-mail something like this (this is an actual e-mail we received, with only the name changed):

> **From**: Meriam _____
>
> **Sent**: Monday, September 16, 2013 10:40 AM
>
> **To**: humanresources
>
> **Subject**: My Resume
>
> Hello HR,
>
> I hope you can use this resume for an open position. If you have any jobs open for which I am qualified, please let me know. I have a health care background but can be trained for any position.
>
> Thank you for your consideration,
>
> Meriam

Wow. I am usually fairly speechless about these sorts of efforts at finding work. Needless to say, we have yet to find work for which people who send us e-mails like this are qualified. Make sure you make recruiters' / HR departments' and hiring managers' jobs easy – don't make them spade the earth trying to find a position that will work for you!

## Miscellany checklist

_____ Don't spend so long tailoring your resume that the job in which you are interested closes!

_____ If you are re-entering the work force after raising your children – make sure the hiring manager knows that.

_____ If you are a felon, don't give up – there are still options for employment out there.

_____ Make sure your references will say nice, positive things about you.

_____ Make sure the contact information for your references is correct and up to date, and that they will provide a positive reference for you!

# In Closing

*Sometimes we stare so long at a door that is closing that we see too late the one that is open.*

Alexander Graham Bell

Well, we've come a long way, you and I. We began by discussing our caustic economic climate, then proceeded through the various aspects of successful resume writing until we've gotten to this point. Hopefully along the way you've made some decisions about making your resume the best it can be, and how to give yourself the edge against the considerable competition that exists in today's job search market.

Hopefully, some of the things you have decided to do include:

- Tailor your resume for each and every job;

- Use formatting judiciously;

- Use appropriate resume language (resume shorthand);

- Seek out and use action words and key words;

- Use key words from the job ad;

- Stay positive;

- Work hard (this is your work now – finding a job);

- Keep to two pages!

## THE PERFECT RESUME

As I close out this book, I wish to thank you for sticking with me through the end. Perhaps you already knew some of the things I've presented here; hopefully you were able to glean a nugget or two through all this that helps create a resume that will get you in the door, and will allow you to land that perfect job! Let me know how your job search is going at *wdanielquillen@gmail.com*.

## Appendix – More Resume Samples

In this appendix, we'll provide more sample resumes for you to peruse and hopefully glean some ideas from. We'll provide the following sample resumes:

- Resume for a youth with little experience #1

- Resume for youth with no experience #2

- Resume for a Mom returning to the workforce after years of being out of the workforce

- Resume for an individual who has gaps in his / her employment

- Resume for a Traffic Engineer with some experience

- Resume for National Sales Manager with extensive experience

Following is a short summary of information about each resume:

**Resumes for a youth with little or no experience #1 and #2**

Not everyone has years and years of experience. So I have included two resumes of youth (my son, from several years' ago and the other is a fictional young woman) prior to the time where they had gained much experience. For my son's resume, you'll note that at the time his only real experience came through volunteer opportunities to work in the area he was passionate about. Even though he wasn't paid for this work, the experience was legitimate, and it's something that can and should be included in a resume.

The second example I provided in this area is a fictional youth, although one that has the education and volunteer experiences of several young people I know, and so I concocted a resume with their multiple skills and talents.

For young people: one thing to remember is that if an employer is willing to hire someone who has little experience – a recent high school or college grad, for example – the employer knows you don't have experience. If s/he was looking for experience, they wouldn't be advertising for someone at an entry level. So – don't worry unduly about your lack of experience; but if you do have some experience, even if it's volunteer service, list that.

If there is something you are passionate about, get involved in it now. Veterinarians who are looking for vet assistants love to see candidates who worked or volunteered at animal shelters, horse stables, etc. Dentists love to see candidates who worked as young men or women in dentist offices doing sundry administrative duties.

### Resume for an individual returning to the workforce after years of being out of the workforce

Many women – and men – choose to leave the workforce to raise their children. Sometimes this career hiatus is for a year or two, and other times it is for a decade or two. As mentioned in an earlier chapter, gaps in employment bother me and other HR professionals; however, if I learn the gap was for an individual to step out of the workforce and raise their children, then my concerns largely evaporate.

One concern that remains, however, is whether or not the individual has kept current with developments in his or her field. Whether they are a doctor or lawyer, IT or HR professional, or educator, I want to see something in their resume or cover letter to explain what they have done to keep current in technologies, trends, etc.

By the way, this kind of resume would work for anyone who has been out of the workforce for many reasons – having and raising a family, caring for an elderly parent or child who is seriously ill, etc.

### Resume for an individual with gaps in his / her employment

I once interviewed a fellow who had an incredible skill set that matched a particularly difficult position I was trying to fill. I was concerned, however, about the gaps I saw in his employment on his resume. For most of his career, he would work someplace for a year or two, and then have a gap in employment of one, two and once even three years. Despite my misgivings, I called him in for an interview.

The first thing I did was explore the reasons for the gaps in his employment. I asked him to walk me through each job departure and what he did during the years when he was out of work. He glibly replied that during those times, he was "trying to find" himself. Each time he thought he'd found his true self, he returned to work, only to discover that he hadn't been quite right, so off he'd go again to find himself.

I decided to let him find himself again without my help – I did not hire him. Those kinds of gaps will be difficult to address in a resume. But other kinds of gaps – such as a mother returning to work after raising her children, a mid-career career change, etc. are a little easier to address.

The temptation will be to use a functional resume – a resume that highlights your skills and capabilities, but doesn't show the years you worked at the companies at which you were employed. I would again caution you, that functional resumes are viewed with skepticism by most HR professionals. Better to do a combination functional and chronological resume, as we discussed earlier. Where ever and whenever possible, explain the gaps in employment, either in your resume or your cover letter. Or both.

**Resume for Traffic Engineer with limited work experience**
We'll move from these difficult situations – little or no experience, gaps in employment and re-entry into the workforce after a number of years – into a resume for an individual who is a somewhat recent graduate in traffic engineering, who is seeking to better their lot in life. They have a good education, and are beginning to get some experience under their belt.

Nothing tricky about the resume – it's pretty straight forward. Note even though s/he has a few years' experience, they are not using that obnoxious Objective section. They are sticking with the Professional Summary and a listing of their strengths and capabilities.

**Resume for National Sales Manager with extensive experience**
Lest you think this book is only for those who have limited or no experience, I am also providing a sample resume for a National Sales Manager with many years' experience. You'll see how to present accomplishments in a manner that will attract the attention of even the most difficult hiring managers, recruiters and HR professionals.

## RESUME FOR A YOUTH WITH LITTLE EXPERIENCE, #1

### W. Michael Quillen
His street address, city, state & zip code
His cell phone # and e-mail address

### Summary

Nearly four years of experience in creating sound design and operating sound, lighting boards and shop time. Worked with equipment such as Machie, ETS Express, Shure, Audio-Technica, and others. Over 800 hours of shop time recorded over three years. Theater experience also includes performing in outstanding plays such as Chess, Into the Woods, Secret Garden and Evita. Also Stage Manager for Little Shop of Horrors. Strengths include:

- Leadership
- Customer Service
- Professionalism

- Problem Solving
- Goal Oriented
- Flexibility

### Sound and Light Experience

| Show | Position | Location |
|---|---|---|
| Grease | Designed and Operated Board | Eaglecrest HS |
| Chess | Designed | Eaglecrest HS |
| Anything Goes | Assisted in Operating Board | Eaglecrest HS |
| Count Dracula | Assisted in Design | Eaglecrest HS |
| Evita | Co-Designer | Eaglecrest HS |
| Into the Woods | Designed | Eaglecrest HS |
| Peter Pan | Designed and Operated Board | Eaglecrest HS |
| Prelude to a Kiss | Assisted in Design | Eaglecrest HS |
| Secret Garden | Assisted in Design | Eaglecrest HS |
| Working | Assisted in Design | Eaglecrest HS |
| Lost In Yonkers | Assisted in Light Design | Eaglecrest HS |
| Rumors | Operated Board | Southern Utah Universary |

**Business Television Studio, Sound and Light Board Technician** **June 1998 to**
Lucent Technologies, Greenwood Village, Colorado **August 1998**

# APPENDIX – MORE RESUME SAMPLES

## Awards and Honors

- Outstanding Theater Student Award for 1997- 1998

- Outstanding Theatre Student for Junior class (1996-1997)

- The Michael Landon Award (All-around outstanding Performing Arts Student)

- Outstanding Choir Student for Senior class (1997-1998)

- Worked on a Foreign Exchange program with French Theatre Company (1998)
- One of three students selected to participate in interviewing candidates for new teacher positions at Eaglecrest HS

- Voluntary representative for the Church of Jesus Christ of Latter-day Saints in the Czech Republic and Slovakia

- Fluent in Czech and Slovak.

# AURIANNA ST. PIERRE

www.LinkedIn.com/in/astpierre     720-555-1212     astpierre@email.com

---

## PROFESSIONAL SUMMARY

---

Rising business professional with Human Resources experience and studies. Strong, creative team player looking to make a contribution to the bottom line. Fluency in multiple languages (English, Spanish and German, with a smattering of Italian) provides an additional dimension that allows great flexibility. Strengths include:

- **Driven to succeed**
- **Enthusiasm**
- **HR Compliance**
- **Creativity**
- **Team Player**
- **Problem Solver**
- **Customer Service**
- **Self-Starter**
- **MS Office**

---

## EDUCATION

---

**Bachelor of Science**, Business Administration with Human Resources specialization, 3.8 GPA, magna cum laude
Brigham Young University, Provo, Utah

---

## LEADERSHIP SKILLS & ACCOMPLISHMENTS

---

**Volunteer Server**                                               **2004 to 2011**
Denver Rescue Mission
  • Volunteer server at rescue mission, providing hot meals to homeless individuals on weekends and holidays. Averaged 25 days of volunteer service per year between 2004 and 2011.

  • Selected to lead other volunteers in providing services. Many volunteers were older and had more years' experience.

  • Proposed ways to more efficiently feed over 200 people each meal. Changes resulted in less wasted food, and 20% quicker service to guests.

**Explorer Scout**                                                 **2008 to 2010**
Boy Scouts of America
  • Participated in ride-alongs with Police officers of the City of Aurora, Colorado to learn the day-to-day duties of Police officers.

• Selected to lead team of citizen volunteers assisting in fingerprinting individuals at the city.

• Assisted Fire Department personnel in inspecting baby car seats and in providing annual "Bike Rodeo" designed to teach young children bicycle and street safety.

**Gold Award Recipient**                                           **2006 to 2009**
Girls Scouts of the USA
 • (The Gold Award is the Girl Scout equivalent to the Eagle rank in Boy Scouts.)

• Complete 30 hours of leadership training and demonstration.

• Completed over 50 hours of career exploration; careers researched and investigated included Human Resources, Finance and Banking, Non-profit, City government, Public Safety (Police and Fire), and software development.

• Developed and implemented a community service project to provide toiletries and other personal items to women's shelters. Required to lead other Girl Scouts, leaders and community members in the project, which totaled more than 100 person-hours.

## AWARDS & HONORS

• Selected as Girl Scout troop representative to National Girl Scout Conference.
• Winner of several academic scholarships and one scholarship for exemplary volunteerism.

• Named Volunteer of the month three times by the Denver Rescue Mission and once by the City of Aurora, Colorado.

• National Spelling Bee representative from the State of Colorado, 2007

• Graduated magna cum laude with 3.8 GPA.

## RESUME FOR A MOM RETURNING TO THE WORKFORCE AFTER YEARS OF BEING OUT OF THE WORKFORCE

# Annie P. Garcia

Annie's LinkedIn profile
Cell: 720-555-1212
AnnieG@noplace.com

### SUMMARY

Administrative professional returning to work after taking time off to raise her family. Adaptable, energized employee with a penchant for excellence and a can-do attitude and drive. Experienced office manager and supervisor, ready to resume her career and assist a company to meet and exceed their goals and objectives.

- Office management
- Highly organized
- Self-motivated
- Microsoft Office
- Multi-tasking
- Interpersonal skills
- Westlaw
- Proofreading skills
- Time management

### PROFESSIONAL EXPERIENCE

**Stayed home to raise family**                                     **2006 – Present**
During the past decade, stayed abreast of technological advances that came into the market. Community College and online courses taken at least twice each year for the past decade to stay current on the Microsoft Office suite of software. Proficient in and comfortable with all Microsoft Office applications.

**Office Manager / Legal Assistant**                          **2004 – 2006**
Hanson Law Practice, LLP, Denver, CO
- Provided administrative support for one partner and one associate, while at the same time supervising four other administrative personnel.

- Drafted correspondence from attorneys to courts and other attorneys. Attorneys seldom needed to revise drafts that were provided for their signature.

- Performed initial legal research using Westlaw and other research tools.

- Received Employee of the Year award in 2005.

**Office Manager**                                                    **2000 – 2004**
Healing Hands Health Clinic, Aurora, CO
• Managed all front- and back-office employees. Responsible for all hiring, recognition, discipline and termination. Despite previously high staff turnover, retained all staff with no losses for three years.

• Suggested and implemented billing changes that dropped non-payment from 32% to 11% over a two-year period. Given bonus by doctors for creativity and efficiency increases.

• Improved Medicare and Medicaid billing accuracy from 82% to 98%, resulting in quicker payments and increased cash flow for the company.

• Hosted and taught monthly brown-bag sessions in office procedures to enhance the skills and capabilities of the office staff. Morale was high, turnover ceased, accounts payable and receivable saw double-digit improvement the last three years at the office.

**Administrative Assistant**                                          **1997 – 2000**
Healing Hands Health Clinic, Aurora, CO
• Responsible for greeting patients, providing doctors with patient files.

• Created a methodology for scheduling patients and doctors that increased the number of patients doctors could see in a given day, limiting unproductive time for doctors, and cutting patient wait time by 50%.

• Updated patient files, ensuring accuracy and protection of personal health information.

## EDUCATION

Bachelor of Science in Business Administration, Metropolitan State College of Denver (summa cum laude)

## RESUME FOR AN INDIVIDUAL WHO HAS GAPS IN HIS / HER EMPLOYMENT

# Chris Hannigan

Chris's LinkedIn profile
Cell: 630-555-1213
CLHannigan@noplace.com

---

## SUMMARY

Experienced business professional seeking a change of profession after nearly fifteen years in the workforce. Strong analytical, customer service, sales and writing skills, along with a drive for professionalism and excellence are highlights of this business professional.

---

## PROFESSIONAL SKILLS

*Communication*

- Outstanding written and oral communication skills
- Diplomatic and tactful
- Able to work effectively with children as well as adults, with blue-collar workers as well as C-suite executives

*Sales*

- Received New Car Salesperson of the Year award four out of five years (award presented to top salesperson out of 33 sales people)
- Recognized with Integrity Award thirteen of 19 quarters at dealership (Integrity was always expected… Integrity Award given to top 15% of sales personnel who demonstrated integrity above and beyond expectations during the quarter)
- Recipient of dozens of customer compliments during five years at dealership
- Highest sales margin on new cars sold three of five years

*Management*

- Provided store leadership for medium-size retail store for three years

- Managed the sales activities of twenty-one sales personnel as well as being responsible for all store accounts payables and accounts receivables
- Store exceeded parent company's sales goals every year from 108% to 122%

*Teaching*

- Taught fourth- and fifth-grade children four years
- In three of four years, every student was proficient in reading, science and math. In the one year missed, only one child was below proficient, and that just barely. (Tutored child during the summer so he was proficient in all three areas prior to fall semester beginning.)

*Analytical*

- Evaluated accounts payable and receivable processes and found them less than efficient. Introduced new tools and processes, increasing receivables 19% over two-year period and maximizing float on payables.
- Identified ways to increase efficiency by re-allocating work force. Efforts yielded higher sales, larger margins and lower employee turnover. Efforts recognized by two Manager of the Year awards.

---

## WORK EXPERIENCE

| | |
|---|---|
| **Henry's Boutiques, Naperville, Illinois** | **2012 – Present** |
| **Sagin's Nissan** | **2005 – 2010** |
| **Aurora Public Schools, Aurora, Illinois** | **2000 – 2003** |

---

## EDUCATION

**Rutgers University**, BA History, Elementary Teaching certificate

## RESUME FOR TRAFFIC ENGINEER WITH LIMITED WORK EXPERIENCE

# Dusty Donovan

Dusty's LinkedIn profile
Cell: 512-555-1213
DustyD@noplace.com

---

## SUMMARY

Experienced civil engineer with increasingly responsible traffic engineering experience in multiple municipalities. Full spectrum of traffic engineering skills and capabilities have been honed and are ready for further use and growth. ATSSA and IMSA certifications have allowed growth in the traffic engineering arena. Strengths include:

---

- Traffic engineering
- Traffic signal programming
- Traffic engineering standards
- Traffic survey analysis

- Traffic control device modification
- Field measurement
- Engineering drafting
- Engineering design

---

## PROFESSIONAL EXPERIENCE

**Senior Traffic Engineering Specialist**                **2011 – Present**
City of Santa Fe, New Mexico

- Received progressively responsible opportunities with the City of Santa Fe New Mexico in the areas of Traffic Engineering.

- Performed preliminary design on a wide range of engineering tasks supporting the development of highway construction plans, including roadway alignment, right-of-way designs, traffic signals and maintenance traffic.

• Provided analysis of traffic surveys and other traffic movement surveys, and made design recommendations. Design recommendations often accepted with little or no significant modifications.

• Developed and tested advanced traffic signal programming.

**Traffic Engineering Specialist I**                                        **2008 – 2011**
City of Albuquerque, NM

• Led small team of traffic engineers and performed field measurements in multiple locations. Responsible to evaluate and verify field measurements.

• Conducted multiple traffic condition investigations.

• Became primary contact for coordinating with contractors, developers and other government agencies regarding traffic control and traffic engineering.

• Skills recognized by receiving two promotions over three years, from Traffic Engineering Helper to Assistant Traffic Engineering Specialist to Traffic Specialist I.

---

## EDUCATION

**Colorado School of Mines**, Bachelor of Science, Civil Engineering (cum laude)

---

## CERTIFICATIONS

Traffic Control Supervisor – ATSSA certification
Bench Technician – IMSA certification

## RESUME FOR NATIONAL SALES MANAGER WITH EXTENSIVE EXPERIENCE

# Andrew McGilligan

Drew's LinkedIn profile
Cell: 425-555-1213
McDrew@noplace.com

## SUMMARY

National Sales Manager for Lynnwood Robotics for fifteen years covering ten western states. Inherited a sales team that hadn't met corporate expectations for ten years. Managed 150 of the brightest sales professionals in the industry. Created an analytical data base, actively listened to customer needs and understood the strengths and weakness of competitors, and within three years trained and led this talented team to the top. Over the past twelve years, the team exceeded every annual sales goal with average quota achievement of 114% of target. Team was awarded the "Golden Hammer" by the Lynnwood CEO four times for being the top producing sales team in the company. Strengths include:

- Sales Management
- Customer Service
- Sales Strategies
- Leadership Vision
- Robotics Industry
- Sales Tactics
- Sales Analytics
- Product Management

## PROFESSIONAL EXPERIENCE

**National Sales Manager**                                    **2000 – Present**
Lynwood Plastics, Lynnwood, Washington
- Inherited sales team that hadn't met or exceeded sales quota – either individually or as a team – in ten years. First three years were spent creating and sharing vision, training existing account executives and hiring new account executives where needed. Each of those three years, sales increased over previous years. In 2003, each member of the sales team met or exceeded corporate sales quotas, and has done so every quarter since 2003.
- Developed market analytics tool that allowed team to begin sales cycle at the optimum point – optimum for Lynnwood as well as customers. Sales across every industry exploded, and the team saw double-digit sales increases most years.

• During last three years, every sales team hit 125% (or better) of their quota. Turnover among sales force the previous eight years is 4% total.

• Much of the sales increase has come from taking market share from Lynnwood's competitors. Major corporate wins include: City of Seattle, City of Bremerton, Carlsbad, CA, Weyerhaeuser Aluminum, Northwest Aluminum, Coastal Aluminum, IBM, AT&T, Verizon, Oracle, Cisco, SAP, Peet Limited, Navitas, Northern Star Resources, Sirius and Fortescue Metals.

**Senior Account Executive**                                          **1995 – 2000**
Johnson Electronics

• Top-ranked salesman 1996 through 1999; received Salesperson of the Quarter award nine quarters over a four-year period and Salesperson of the Year four years in a row.

• Surpassed sales quotas every year at Johnson Electronics, averaging 123% of objective, despite escalating objectives in three of the five years.

• Led matrixed sales teams of from four to six individuals to meet customers' needs. As a result of working closely with Johnson's customers, identified more than twenty new product requirements for product management, which subsequently became part of the product capabilities.

• Won a major contract with Excelsior, the first-ever victory of several that were eventually won in successive years. Displaced one of Johnson's major competitors in head-to-head competition. Knowledge of customer's needs and the strengths of our products vs our competitors' product was the key to success.

**Product Manager**                                          **1990 – 1995**
Johnson Electronics

• Managed the Refinity product line, at the time Johnson Electronics' flagship product. Responsible for creating and implementing marketing and sales plans for the product family. During tenure, sales experienced a double-digit increase annually for four years.

• Established the first-ever major Users' Group for Johnson products in general and Refinity product line in particular. During two years of User's Group conventions, over 100 new applications were identified for the product line, over seventy of which were engineered into the Refinity product line. Sales of the company's three major product lines soared 512% over four years. Senior management identified the success of the User's Group meetings and input as major reasons for the sales explosion.

• Designed and implemented a Refinity Road Show to take our product to our major sales locations, where some of Johnson's largest customers' were also shown new products in advance of their introduction to the public. Resulting presales far outpaced all expectations.

Previous Employment History Available Upon Request

---

## AWARDS AND HONORS

- Recipient of the *Sales Professional of the Year* award (2015)
- *Sales Person of the Year* award four years in a row (1996, 1997, 1998, 1999)
- Nine *Salesperson of the Quarter* awards over four-year period
- Product managed product line whose sales grew 512% over four years
- First sales person ever to sign a contract with Excelsior (the first of several contracts)

---

## EDUCATION

**Seattle Pacific University**, Bachelor of Science, Computer Engineering
**University of Southern California**, Masters of Science, Electrical Engineering

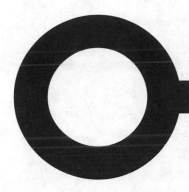

# Index

# INDEX

**Interested in learning how to master social media tools to land that perfect job? Look no further!**

Author Dan Quillen and co-author Dr. Lance Farr have written the only book you'll need to learn the techniques and skills necessary to use the main job-search social media tools – LinkedIn, Google+, Facebook and Twitter – so you can find your dream job. Great price at just $9.95! Available in major bookstores and online through amazon, bn.com, and more.

Dan Quillen & Dr. Lance Farr

For more details on this title, and all our job-search titles, go to:

**www.get-a-great-job.com**